AMOK BOOKS
KALEIDOSCOPICS
BOOK I

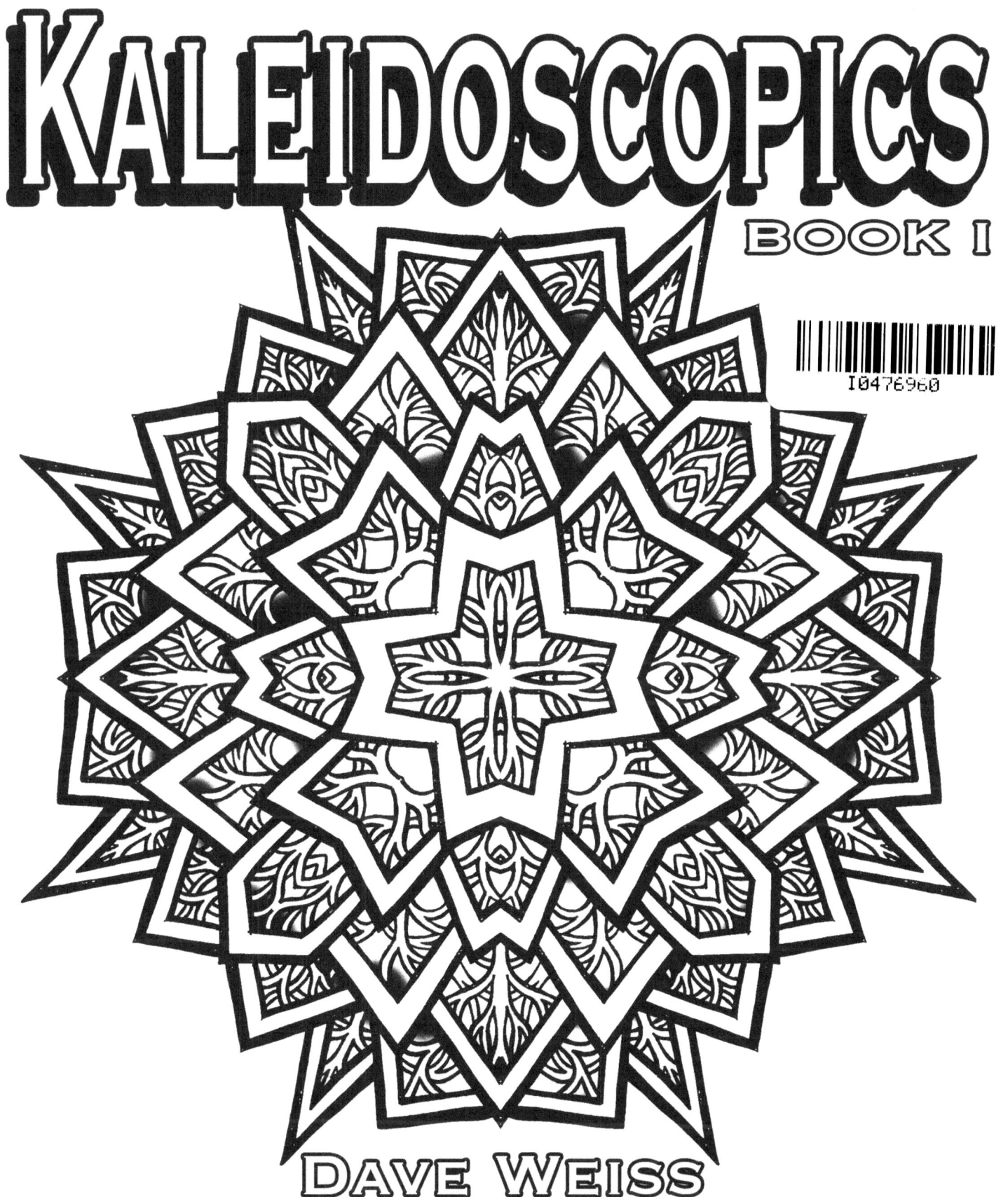

DAVE WEISS

AMOKBOOKS, MOHRSVILLE, PA

DWEISSCREATIVE.COM

Why Kaleidoscopics?

Some people call them Mandalas, but I'm just not comfortable with that. Mandalas are sometimes associated with eastern religious rituals and that's not the direction I'm taking. To me these pieces are a departure from what I usually do. They are created in pieces and cut together into the images you see before you and while I have some idea what the final piece will look like, it is often a very pleasant surprise. It's as if the piece is seen through that favorite childhood toy, a kaleidoscope.

I think of my work on these pages as a kind of artistic jam session — giving my creativity wings and letting it soar. It is my hope that you, the colorist, will do the same. There is no right or wrong way to interpret these, only your way. Have fun with them. Get your materials out and let your creativity take flight. Whether you are coloring just to relax or you're trying to recapture your creativity, know this. You are creative and you are an artist. Pablo Picasso once said, "All children are artists, the problem is to remain one as one grows up."

Welcome back to art. The sky's the limit! Have fun!

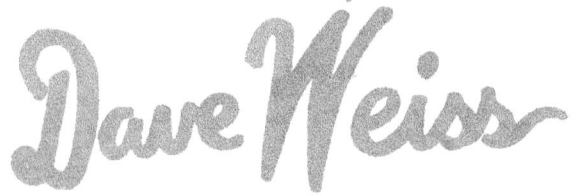

Published Mohrsville, Pennsylvania, by David C. Weiss for AMOK Books. AMOK Books, AMOK Arts and A.M.O.K. Arts Ministry Outreach for the Kingdom are trademarks of David C. Weiss

Illustrations by David C. Weiss, AMOKArts.com

ISBN-13: 978-1522964971
ISBN-10: 1522964975

Library of Congress Cataloging-in Publication Data

Weiss, David C., 1963-
Kaleidoscopics: Book 1, 50 Images to Color by David C. Weiss

ISBN
1. Weiss, David C., 1963- 2. Art
3. Coloring

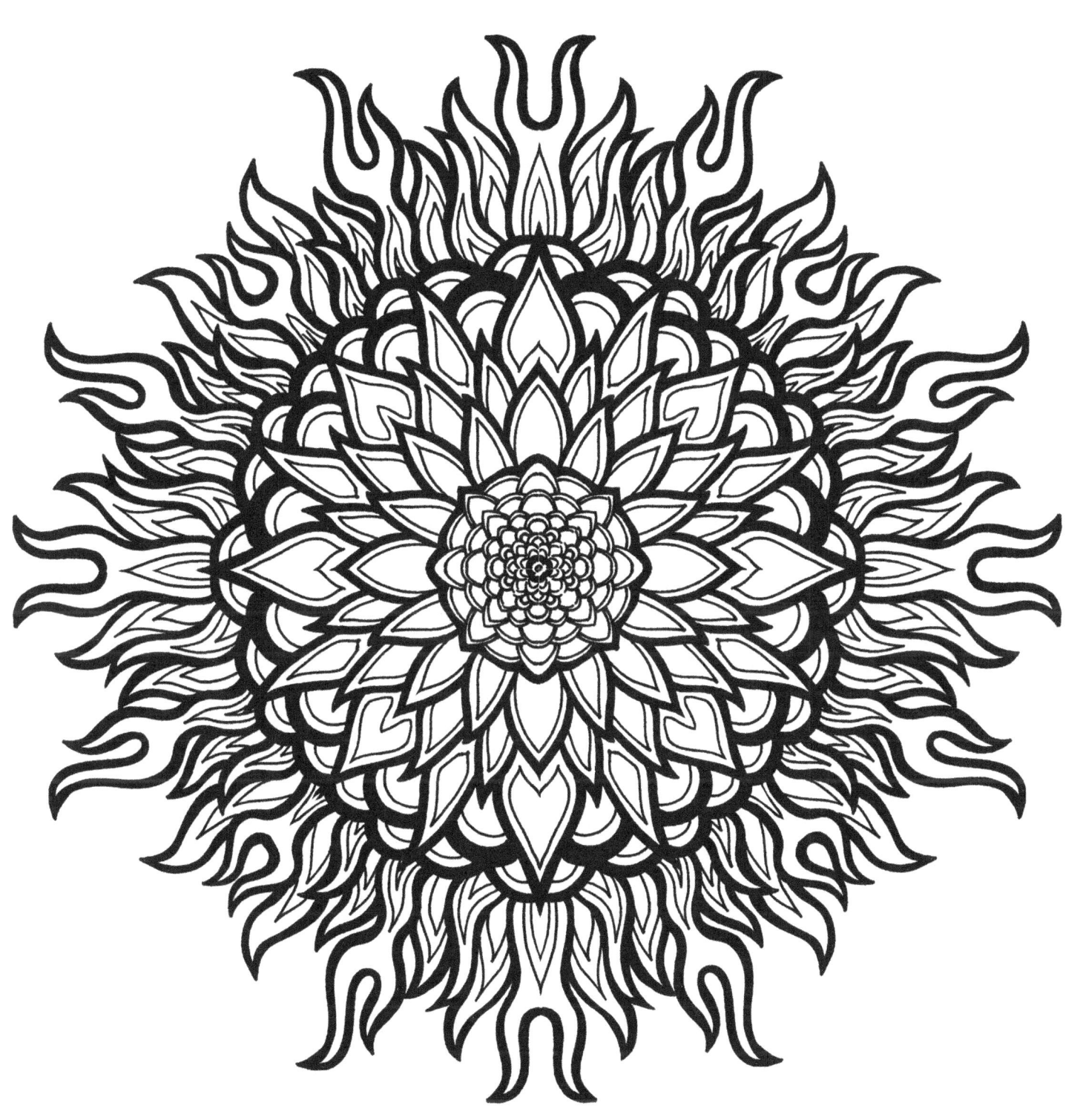

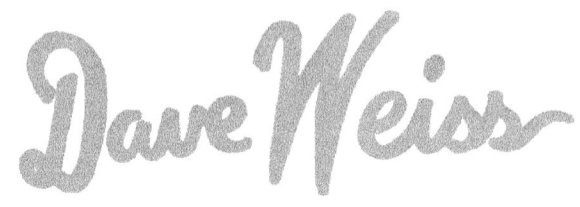

Kaleidoscopics Book 1
"Fireflower"

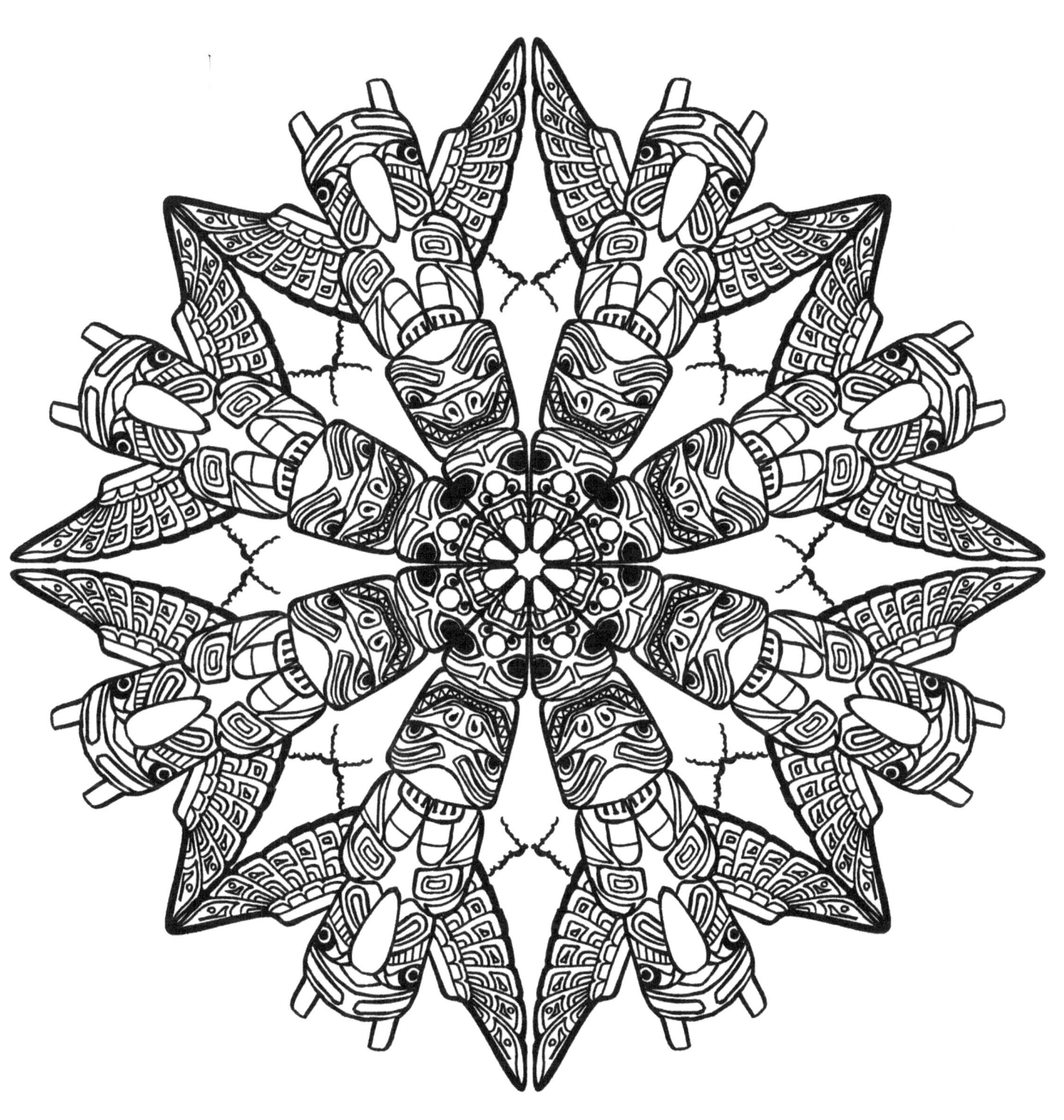

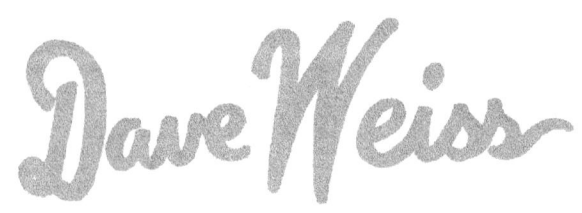

Kaleidoscopics Book 1
"Totem"

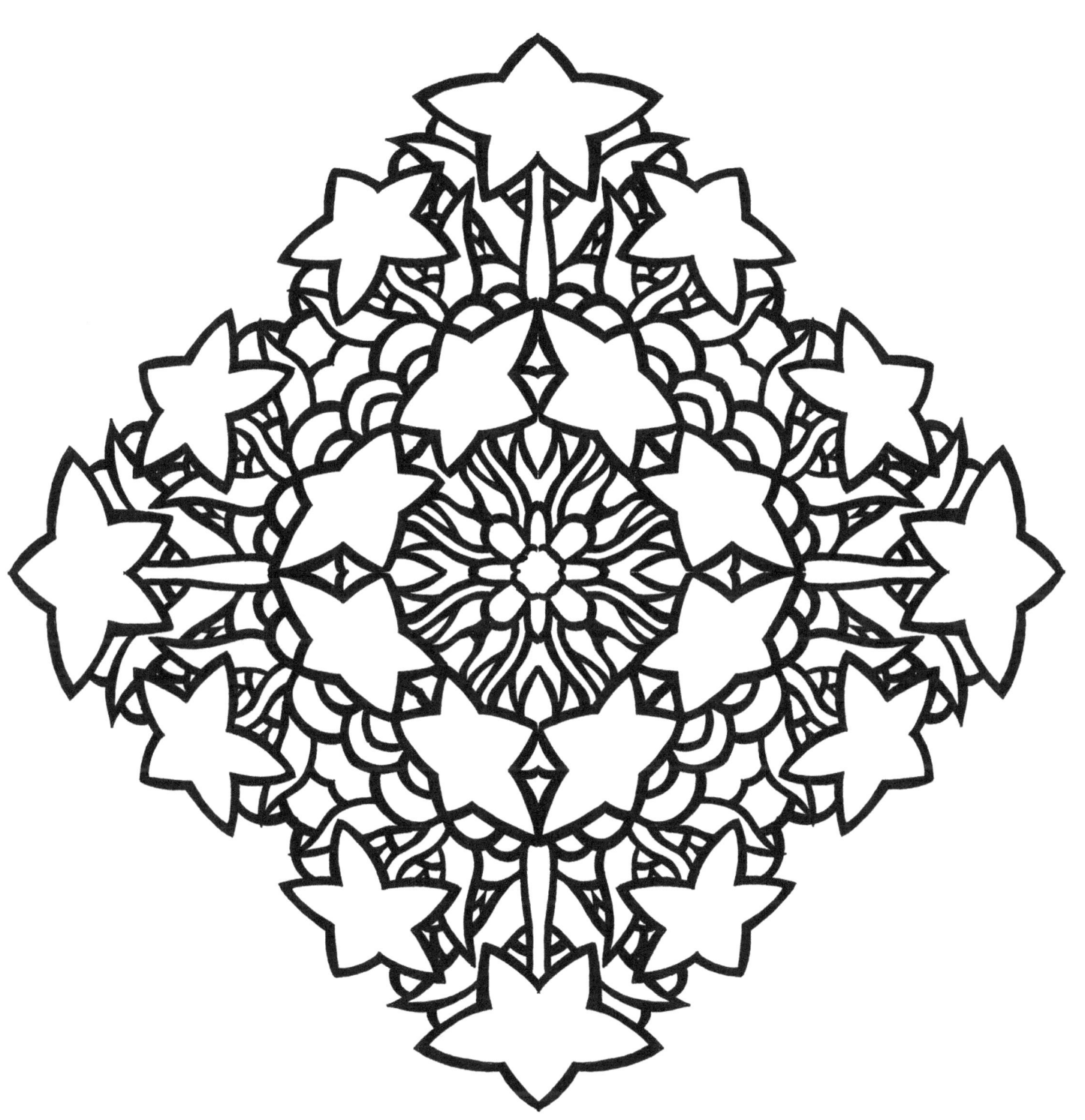

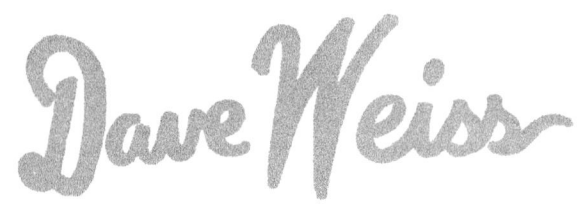

Kaleidoscopics Book 1
"Bouquet of Stars"

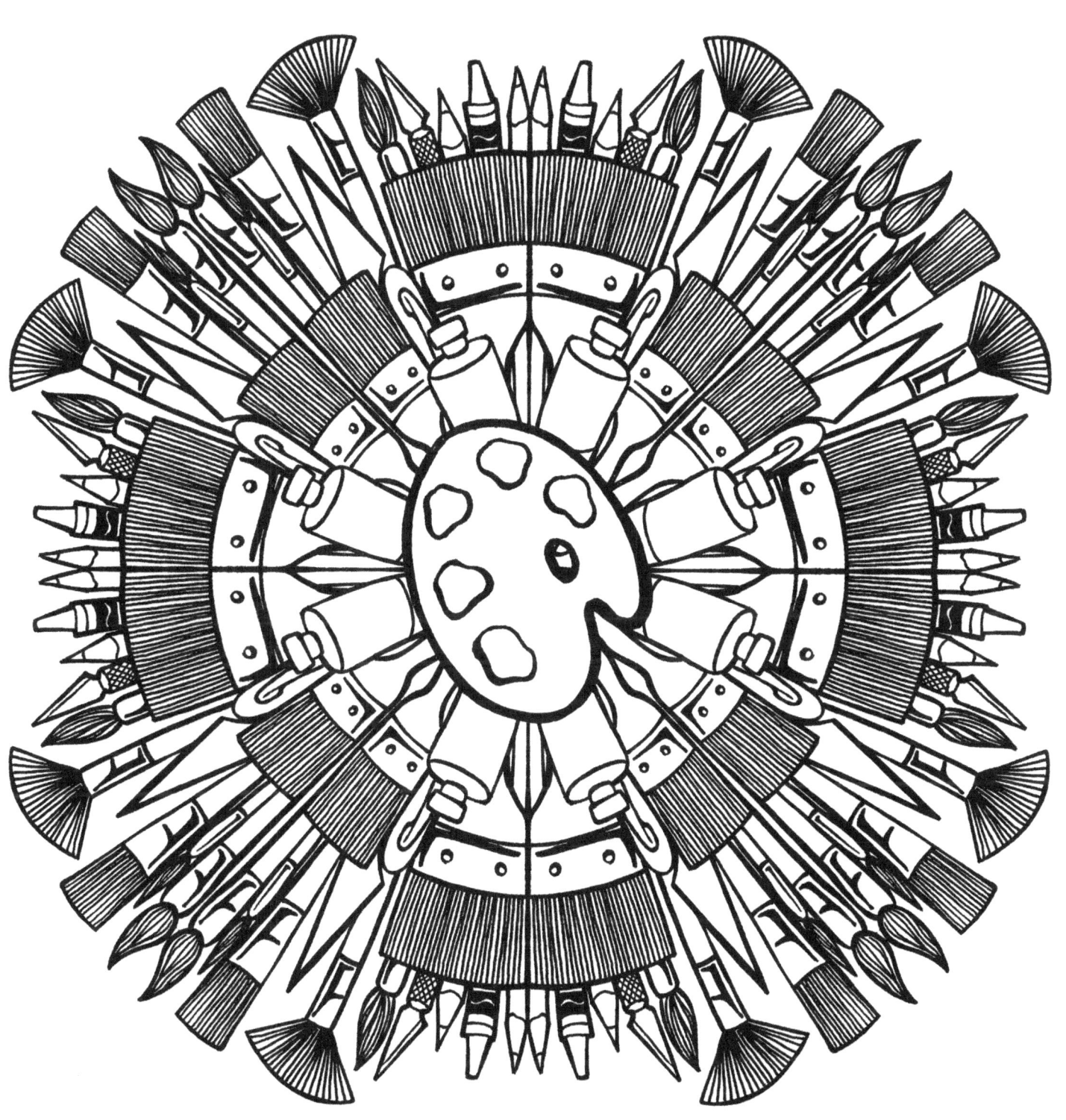

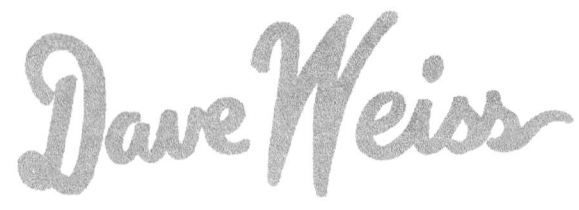

Kaleidoscopics Book 1
"Tools of the Trade"

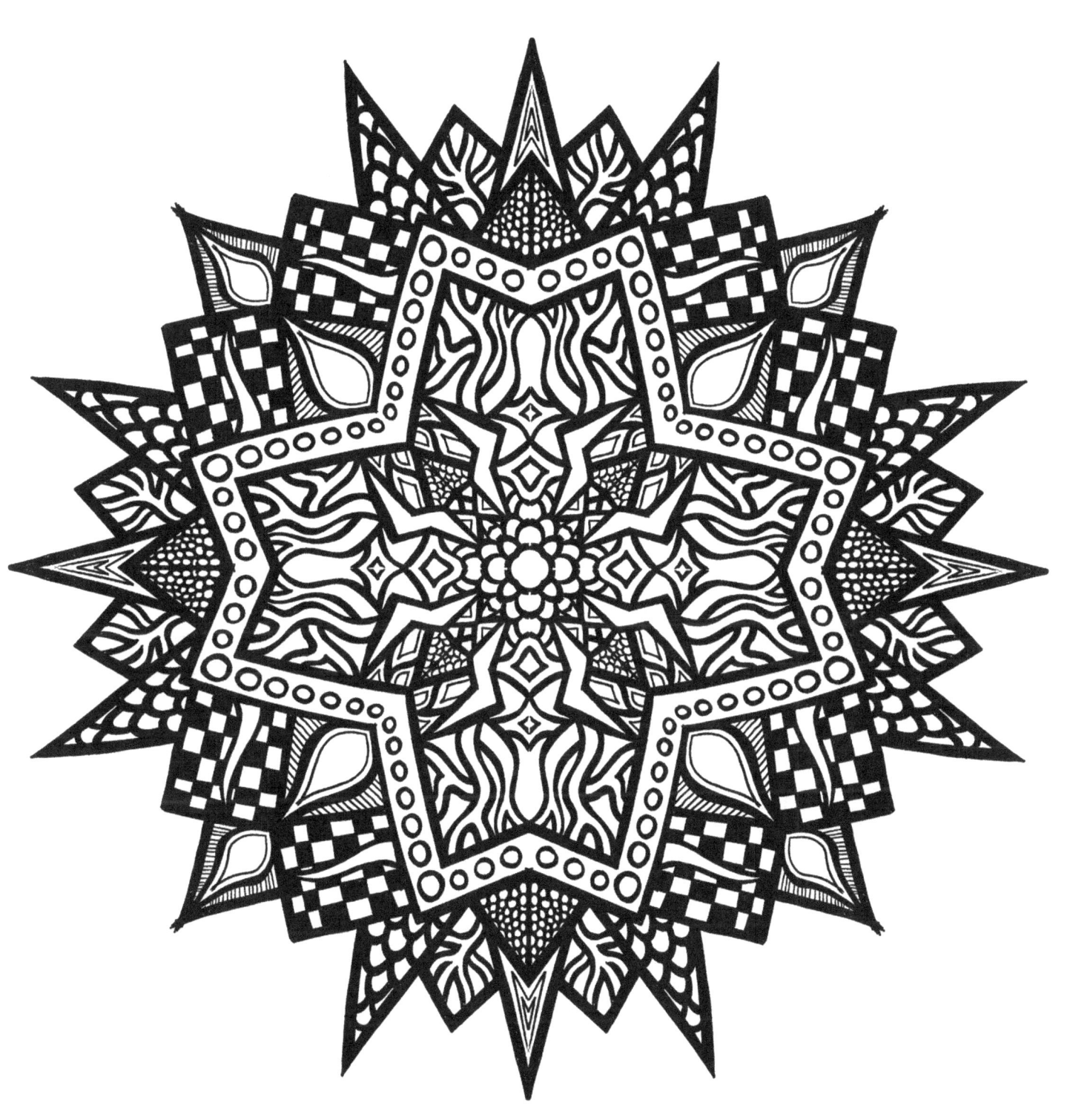

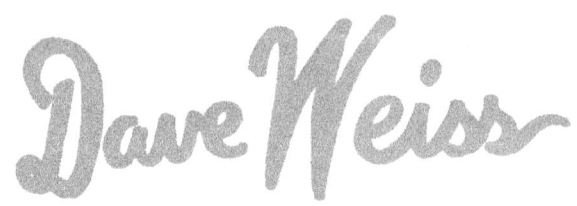

Kaleidoscopics Book 1
"Grande Marquis"

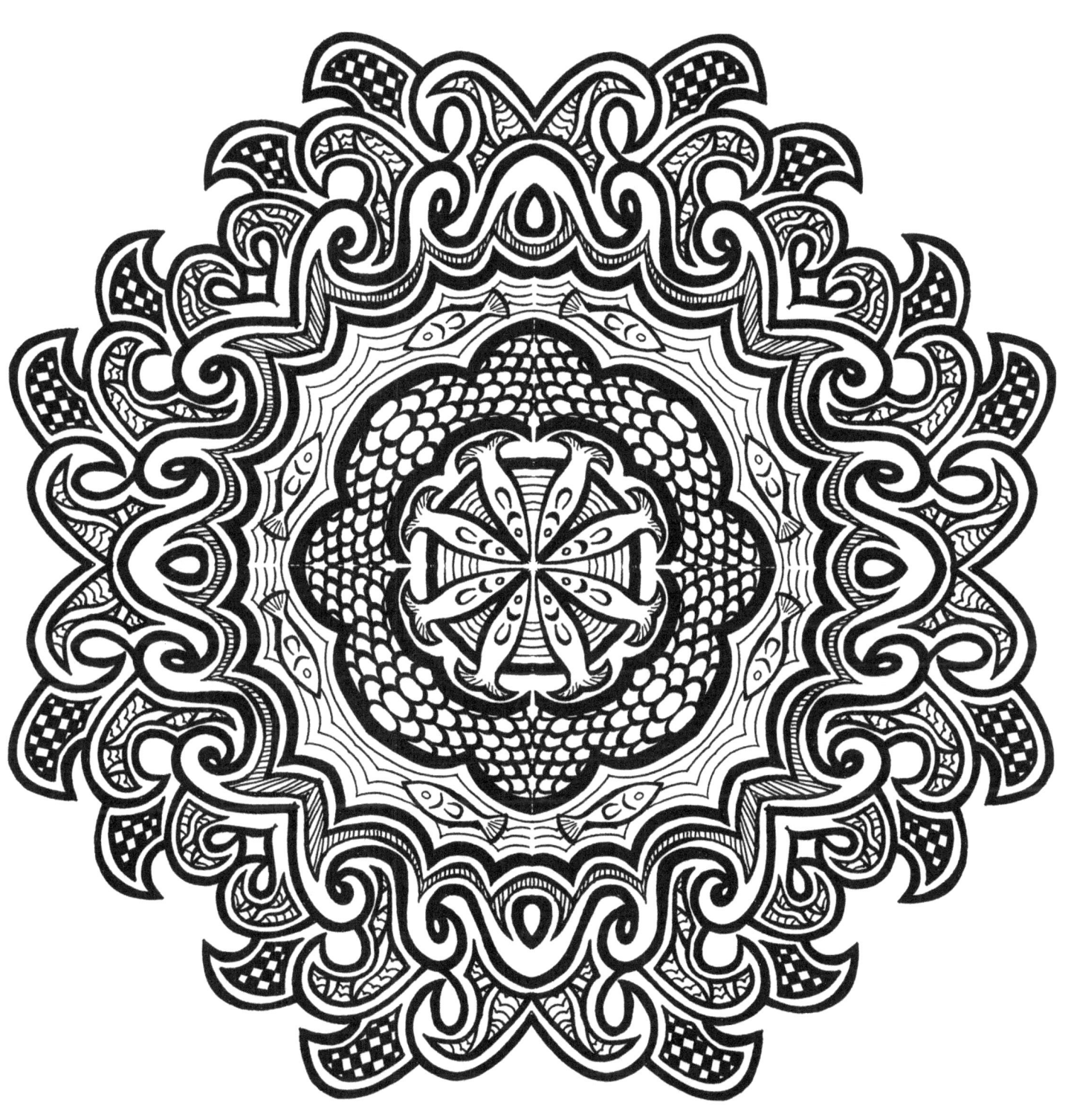

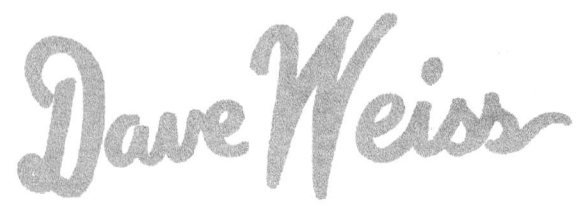

Kaleidoscopics Book 1
"Makin' Waves"

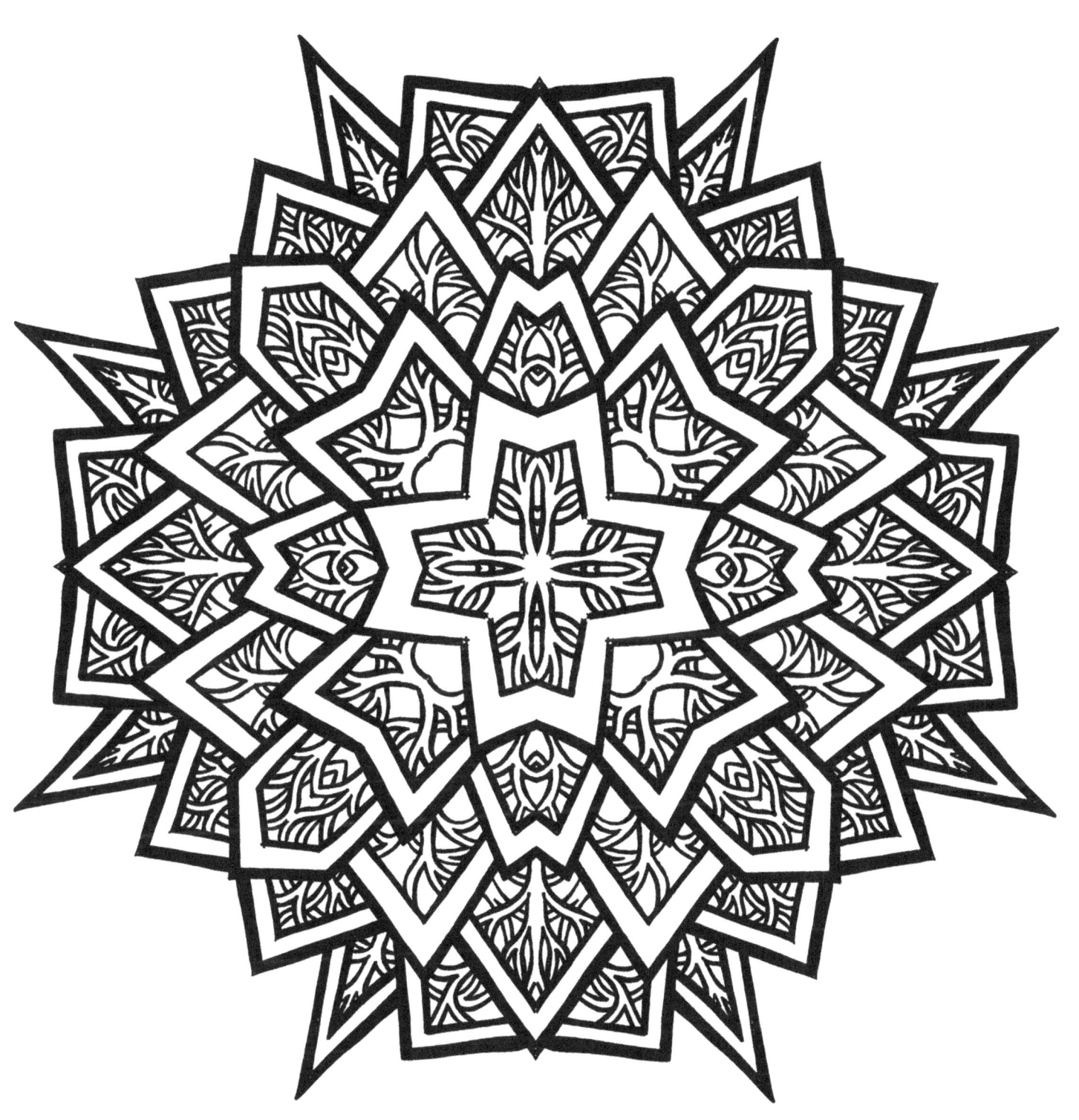

Dave Weiss

Kaleidoscopics Book 1
"Crystal Trees"

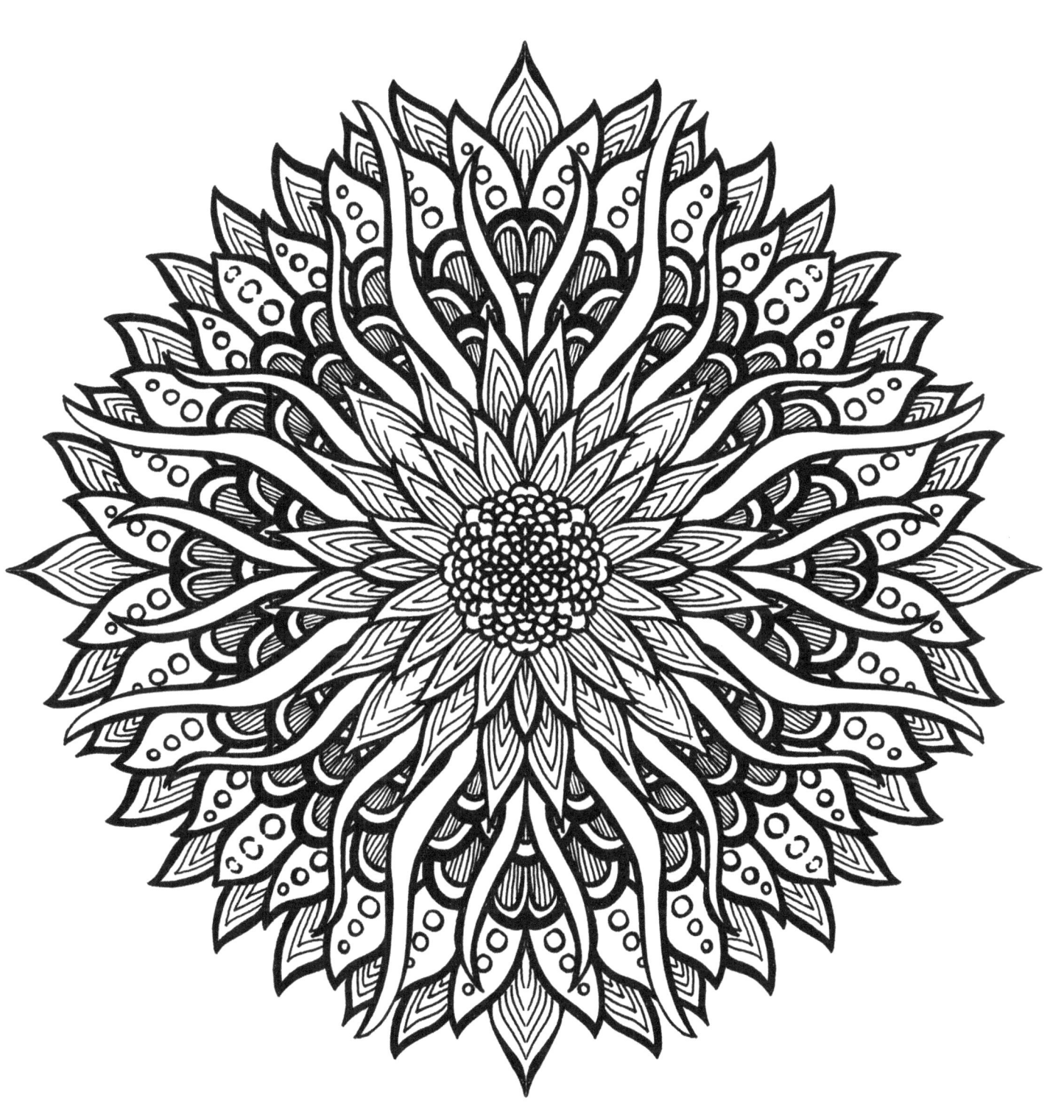

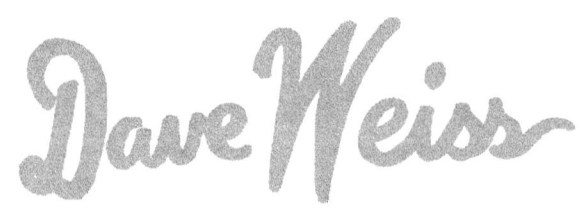

Kaleidoscopics Book 1
"Psycho Psunflower"

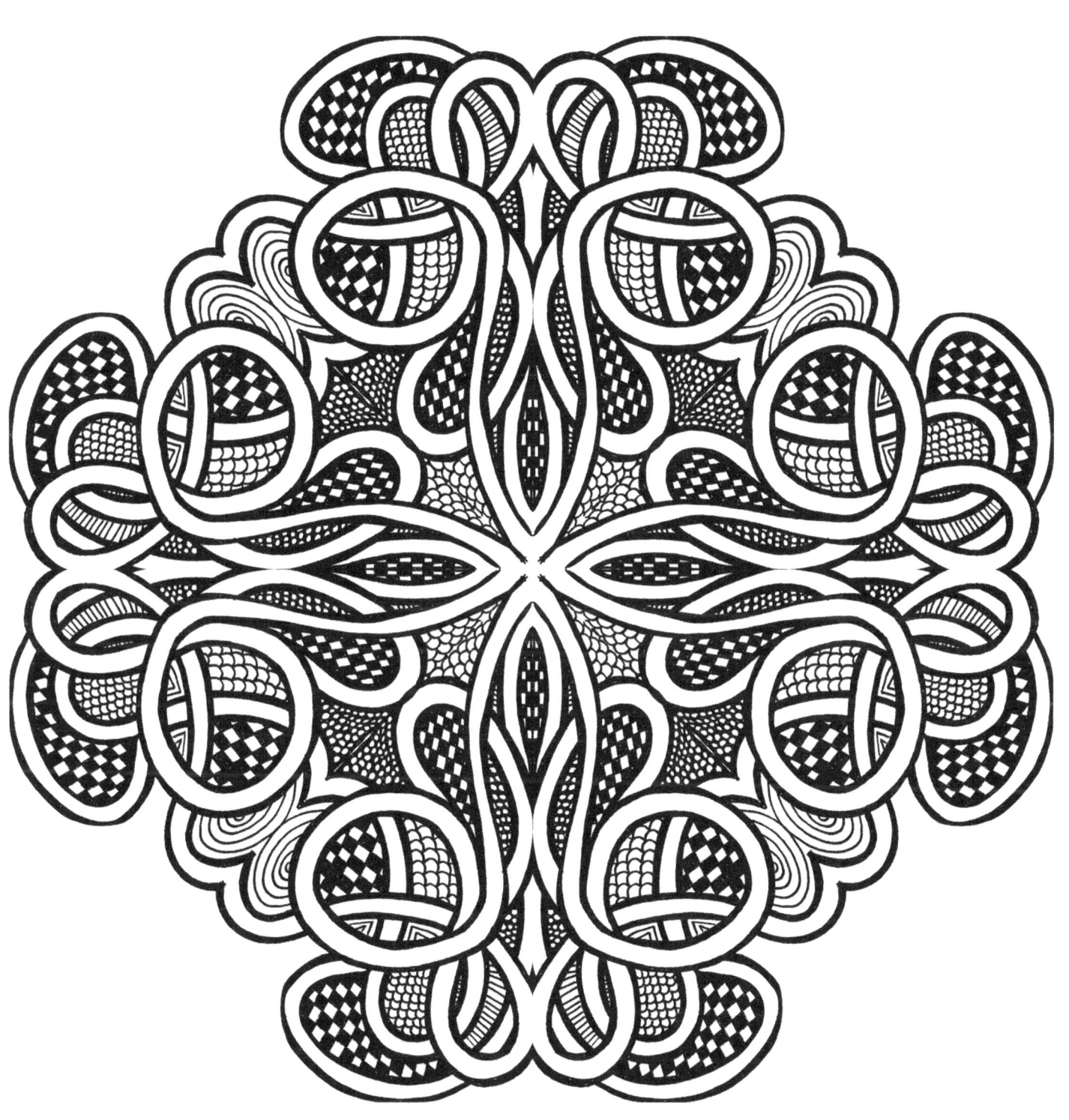

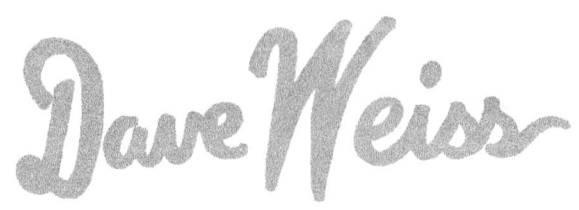

Kaleidoscopics Book 1
"Curls and Twirls"

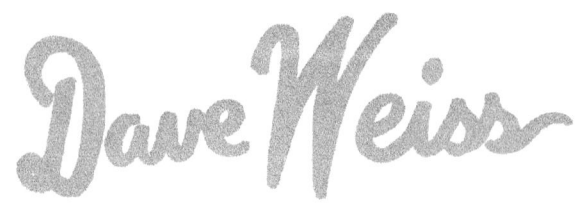

Kaleidoscopics Book 1
"Lace of Spades"

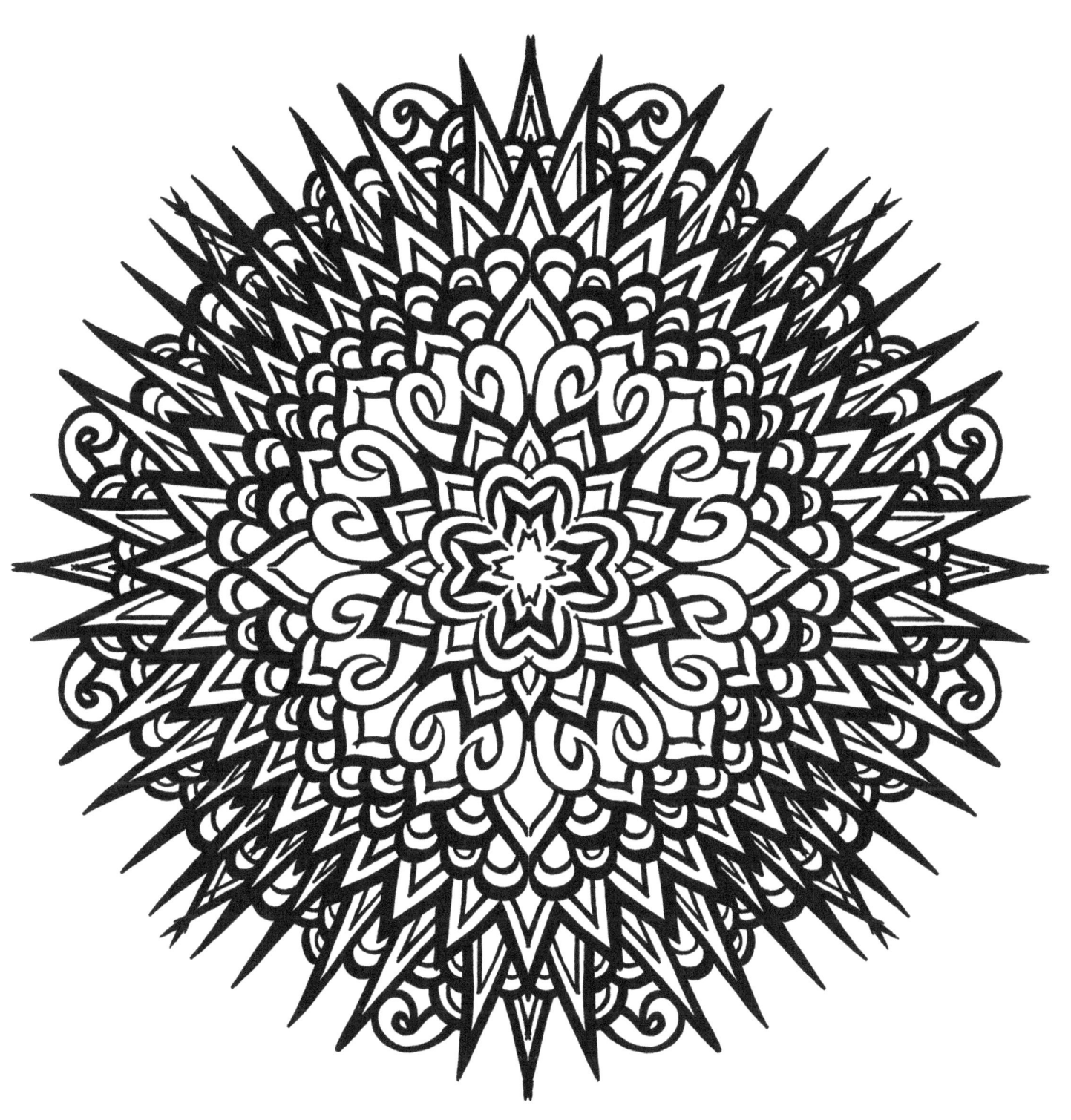

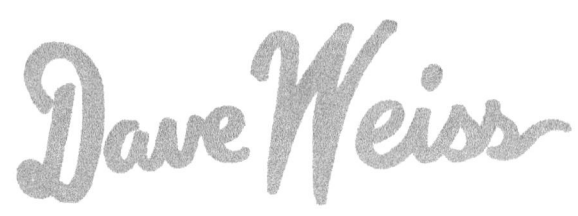

Kaleidoscopics Book 1
"Thistle"

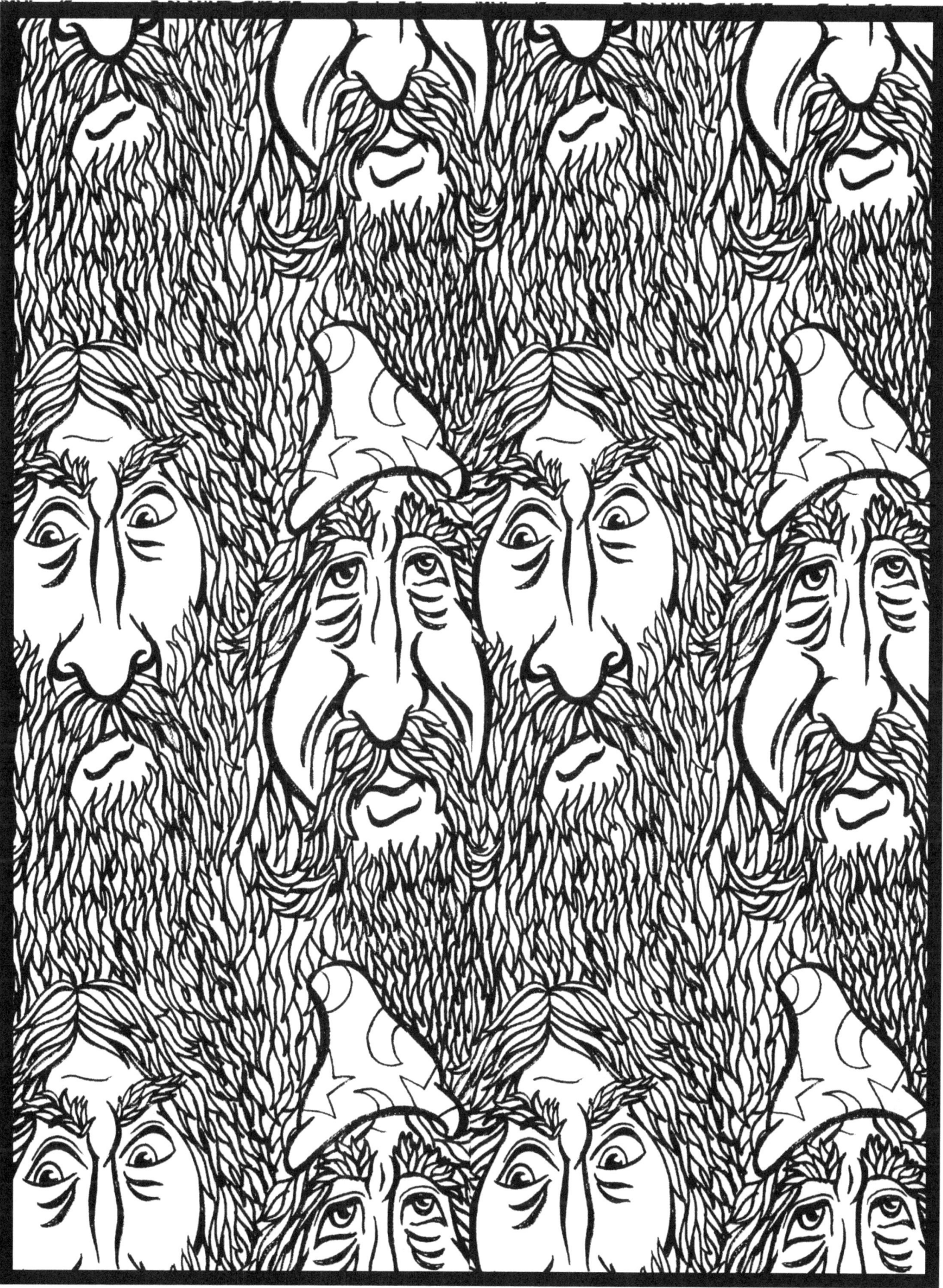

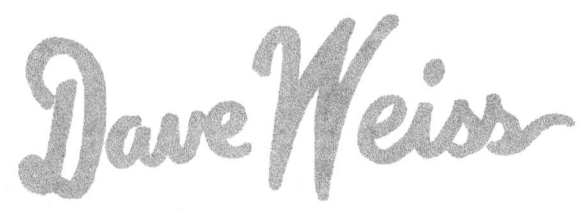

Kaleidoscopics Book 1
"Wizzzin'"

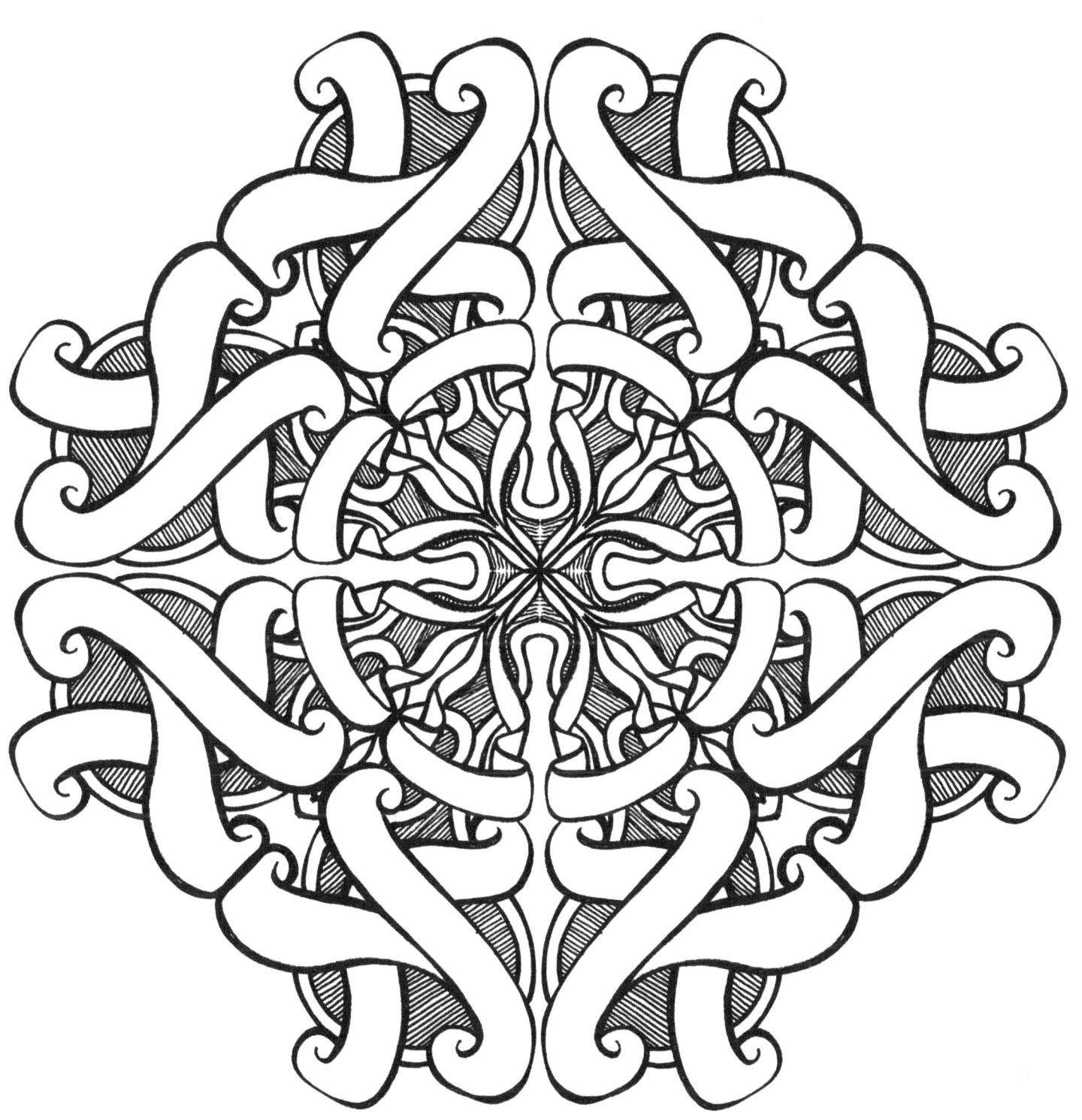

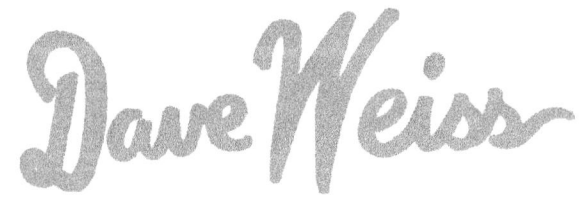

Kaleidoscopics Book 1
"Banners"

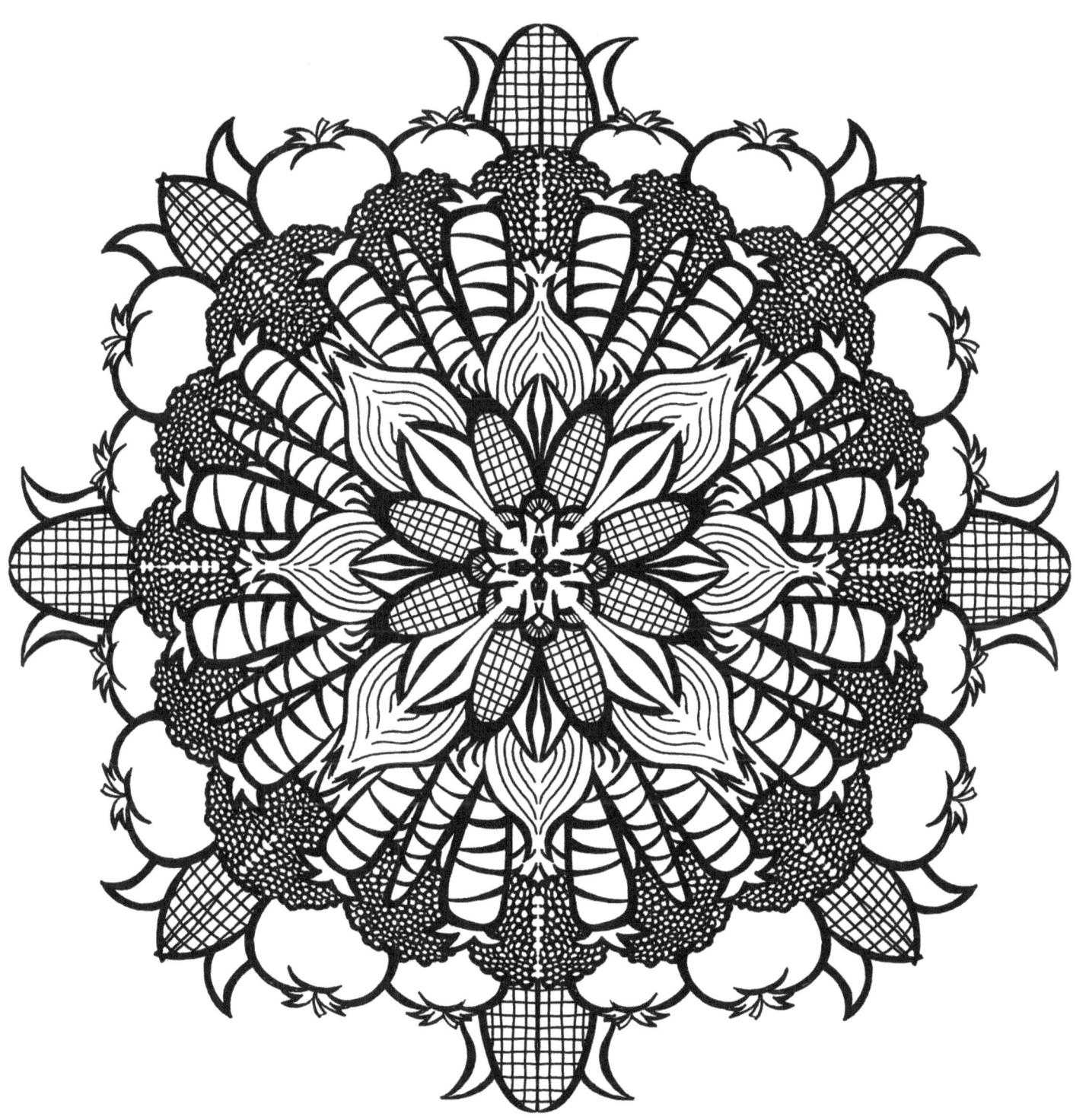

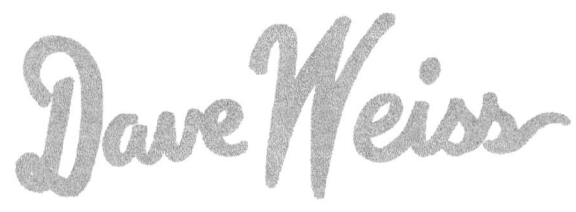

Kaleidoscopics Book 1
"Eat Yer Veggies"

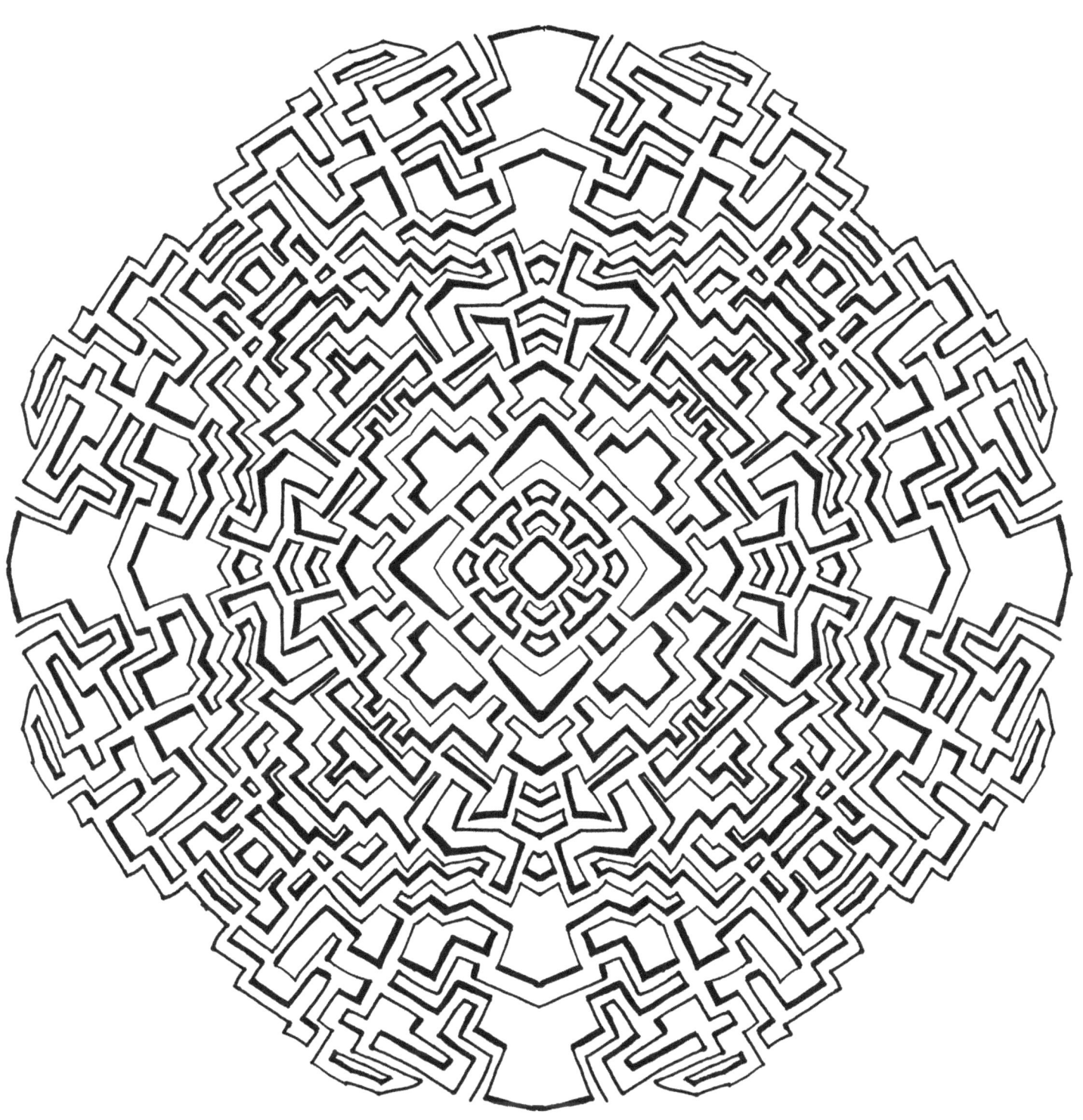

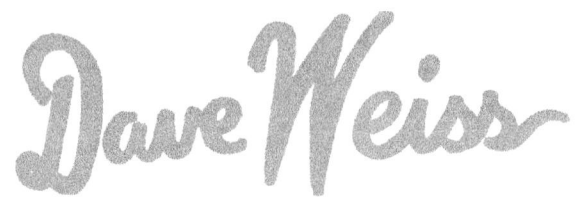

Kaleidoscopics Book 1
"Mayan Maze"

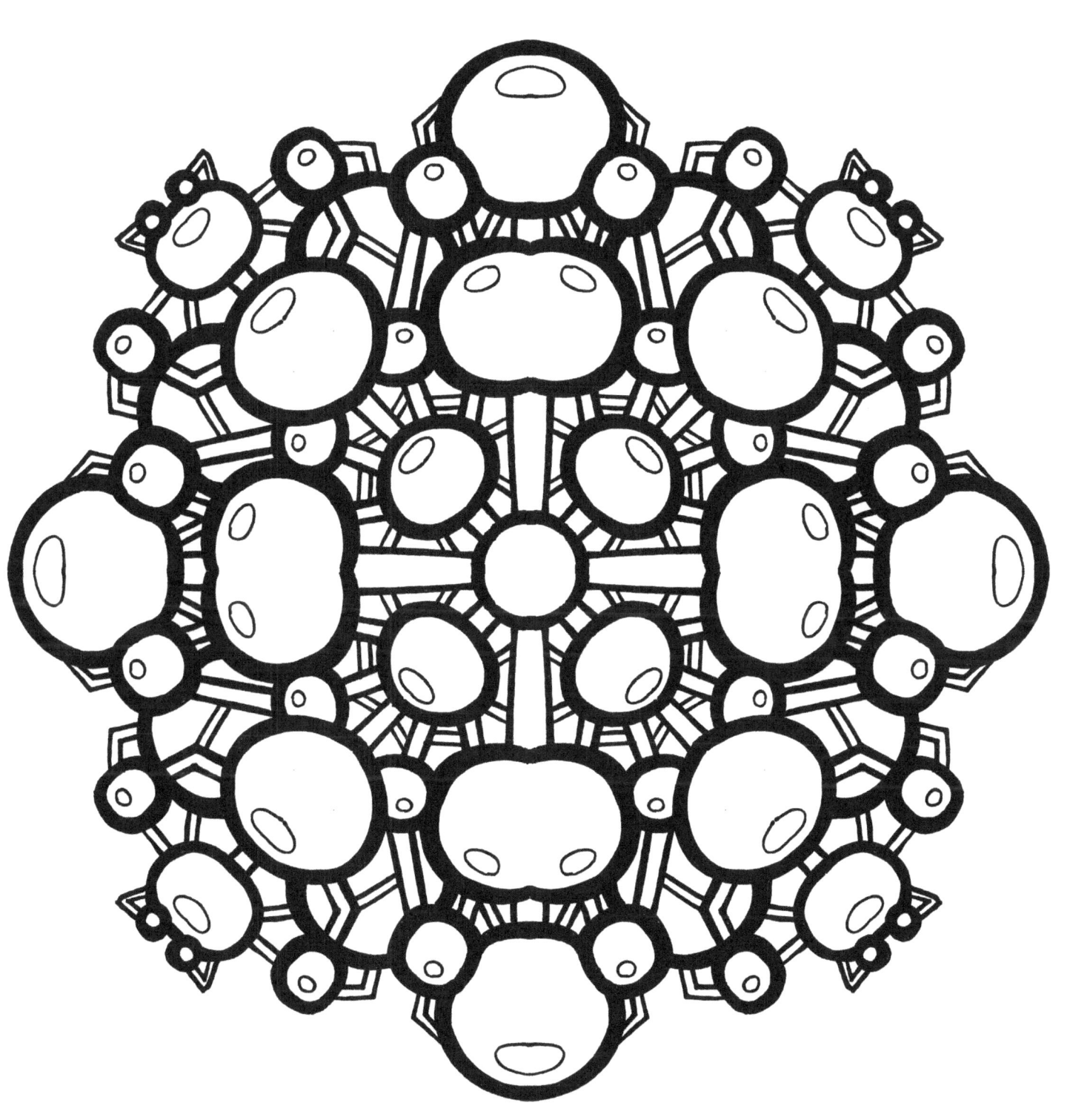

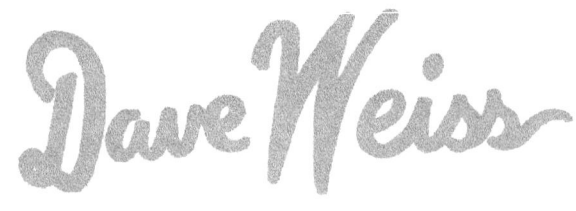

Kaleidoscopics Book 1
"Biosphere"

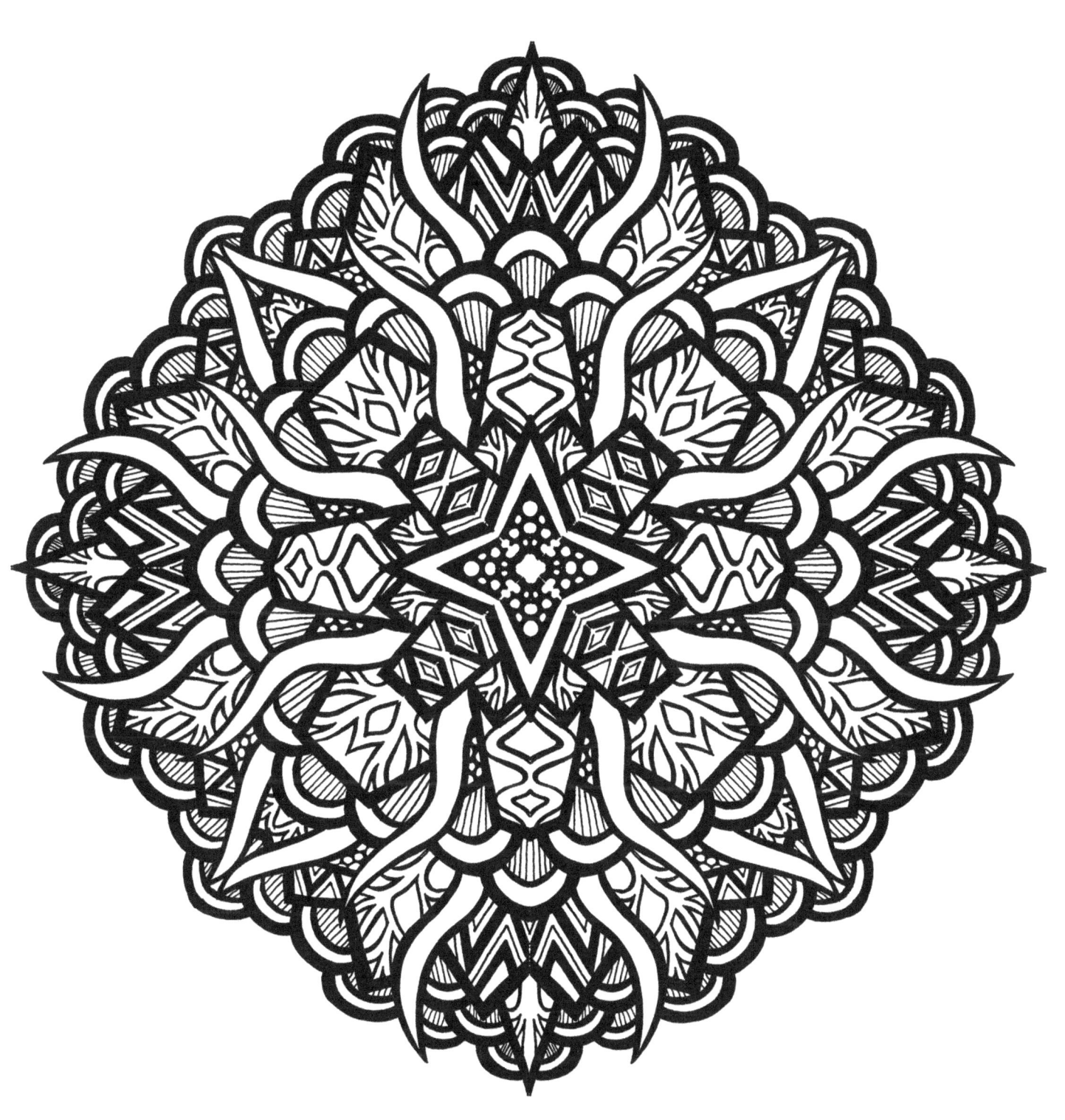

Dave Weiss

Kaleidoscopics Book 1
"Grand Designs"

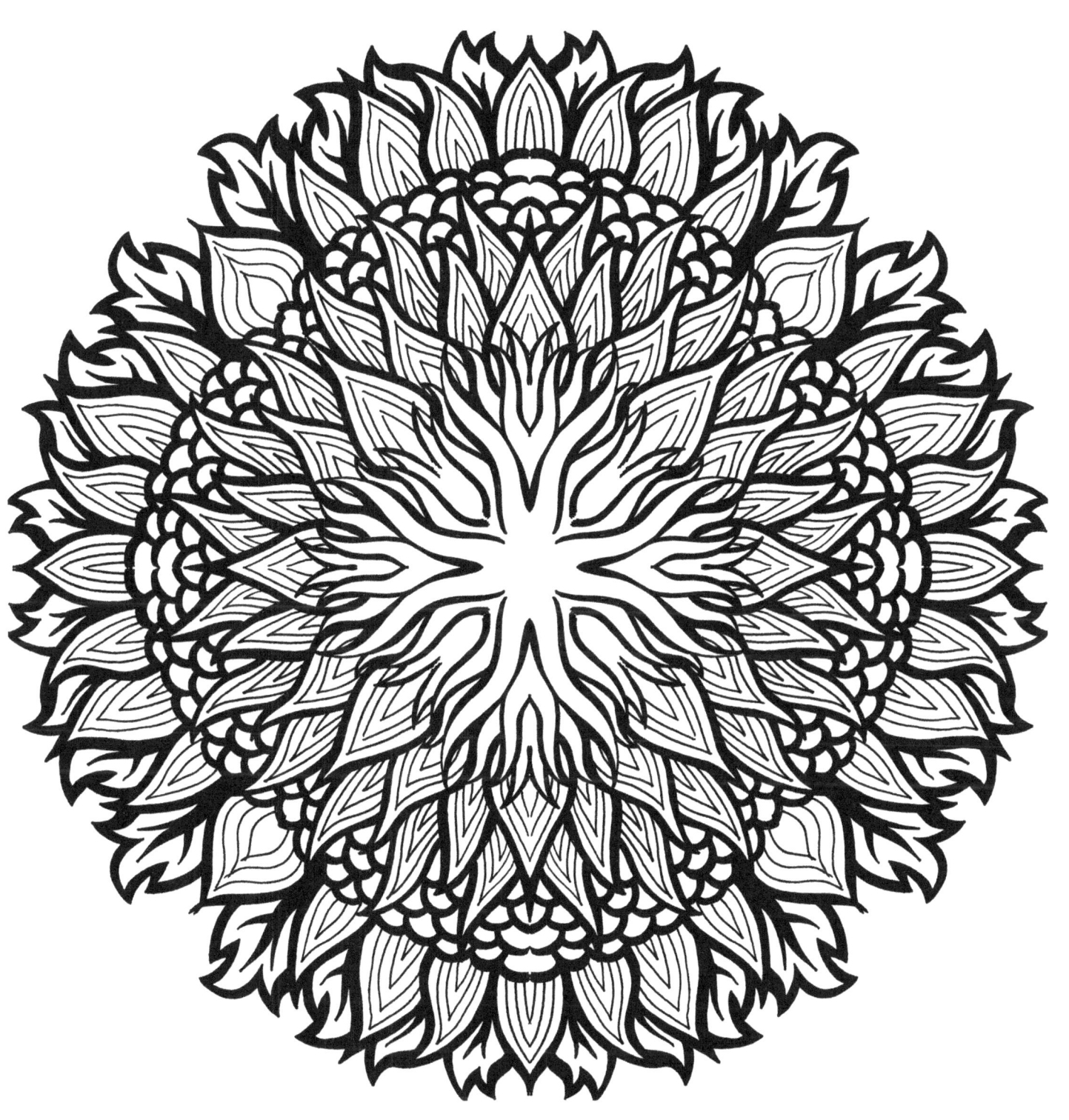

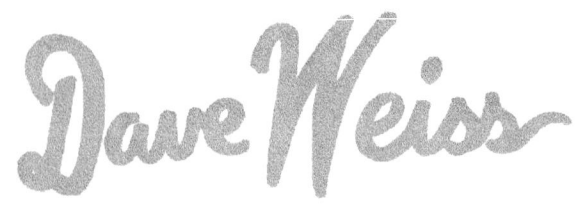

Kaleidoscopics Book 1
"Rooted"

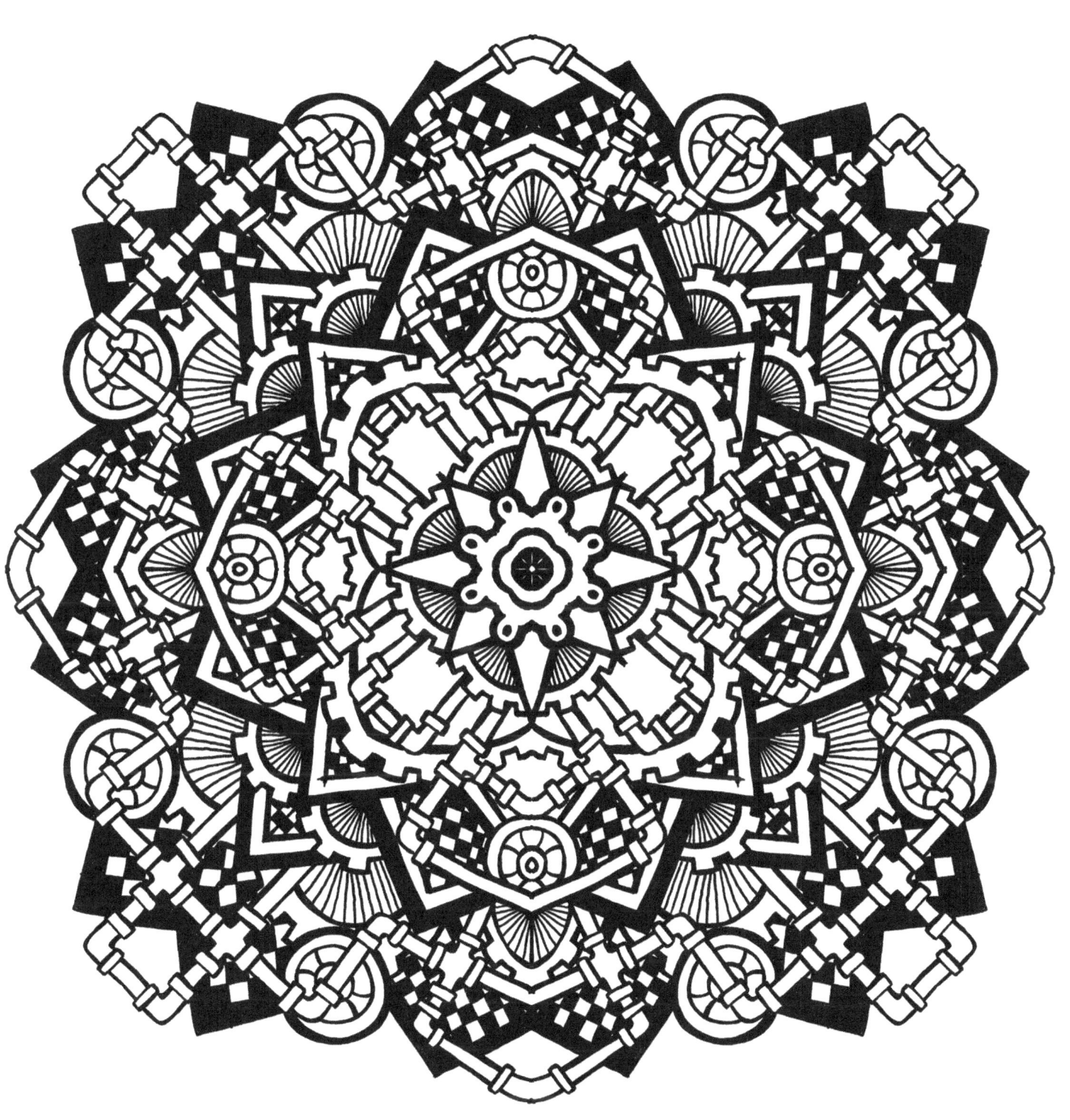

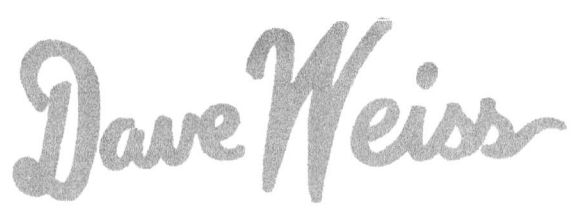

Kaleidoscopics Book 1
"Steam Punk Pipe Dream"

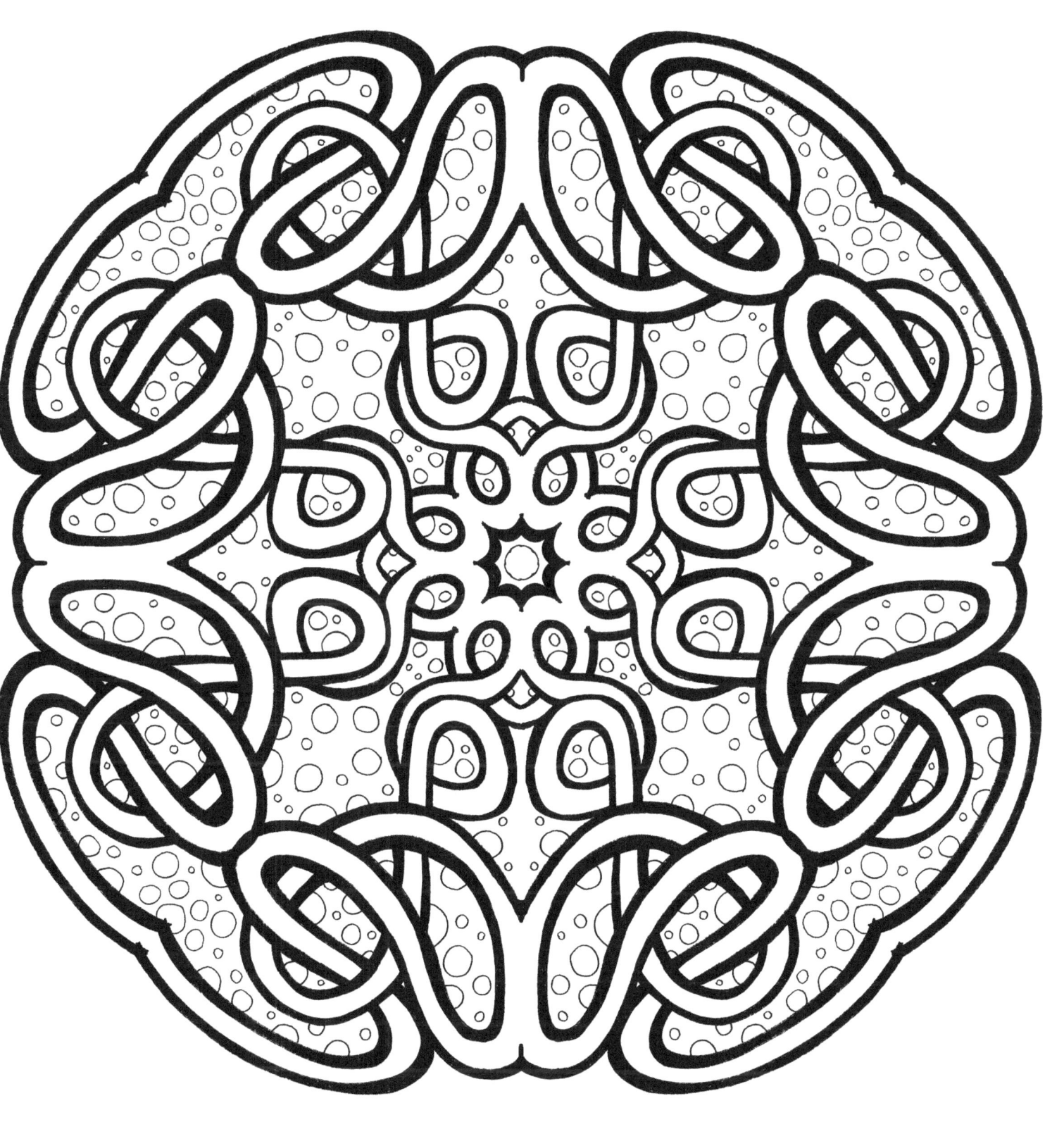

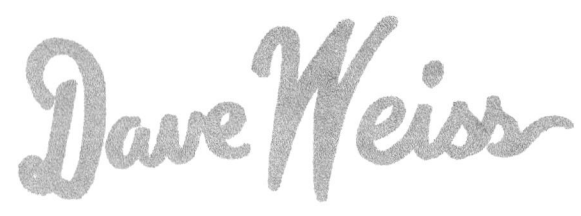

Kaleidoscopics Book 1
"Twisted"

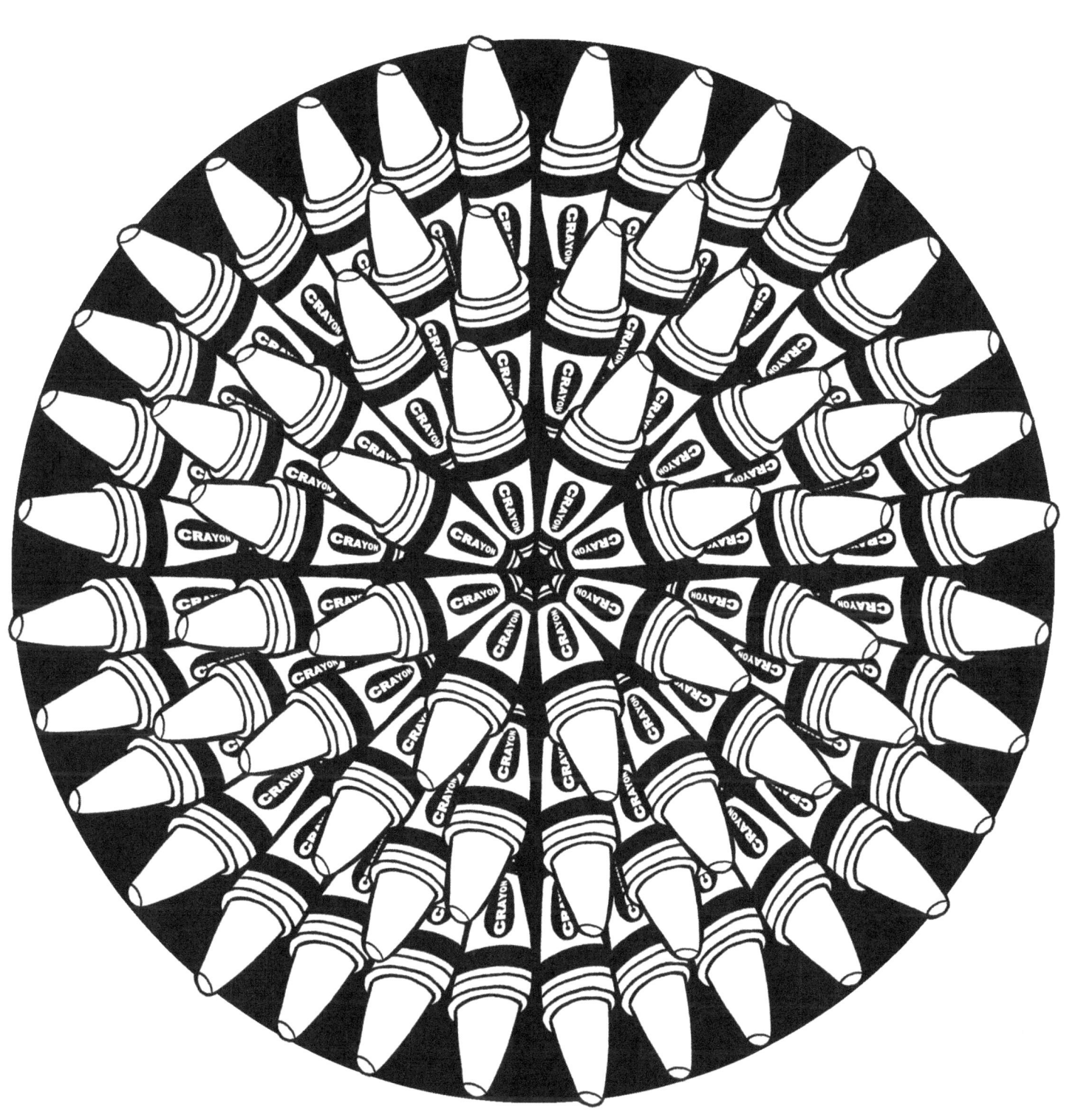

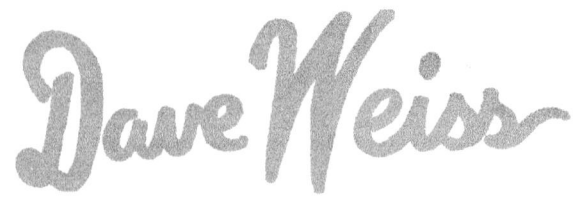

Kaleidoscopics Book 1
"64 Crayon Pack"

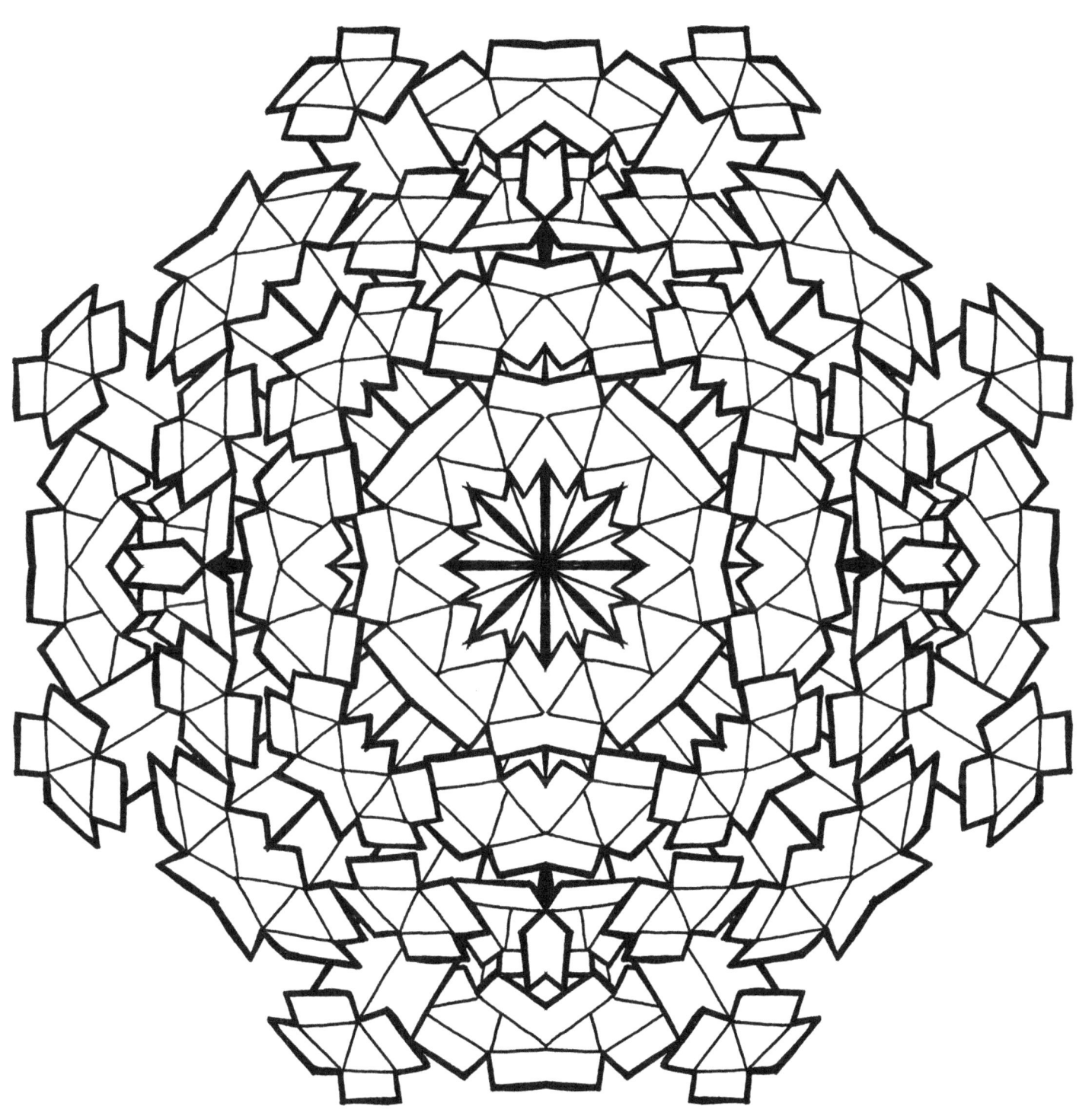

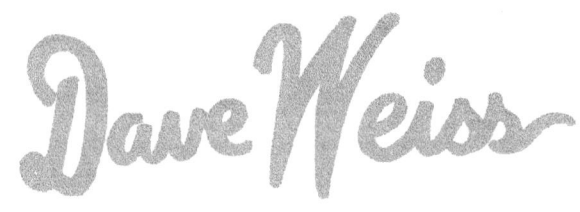

Kaleidoscopics Book 1
"Out of the Box"

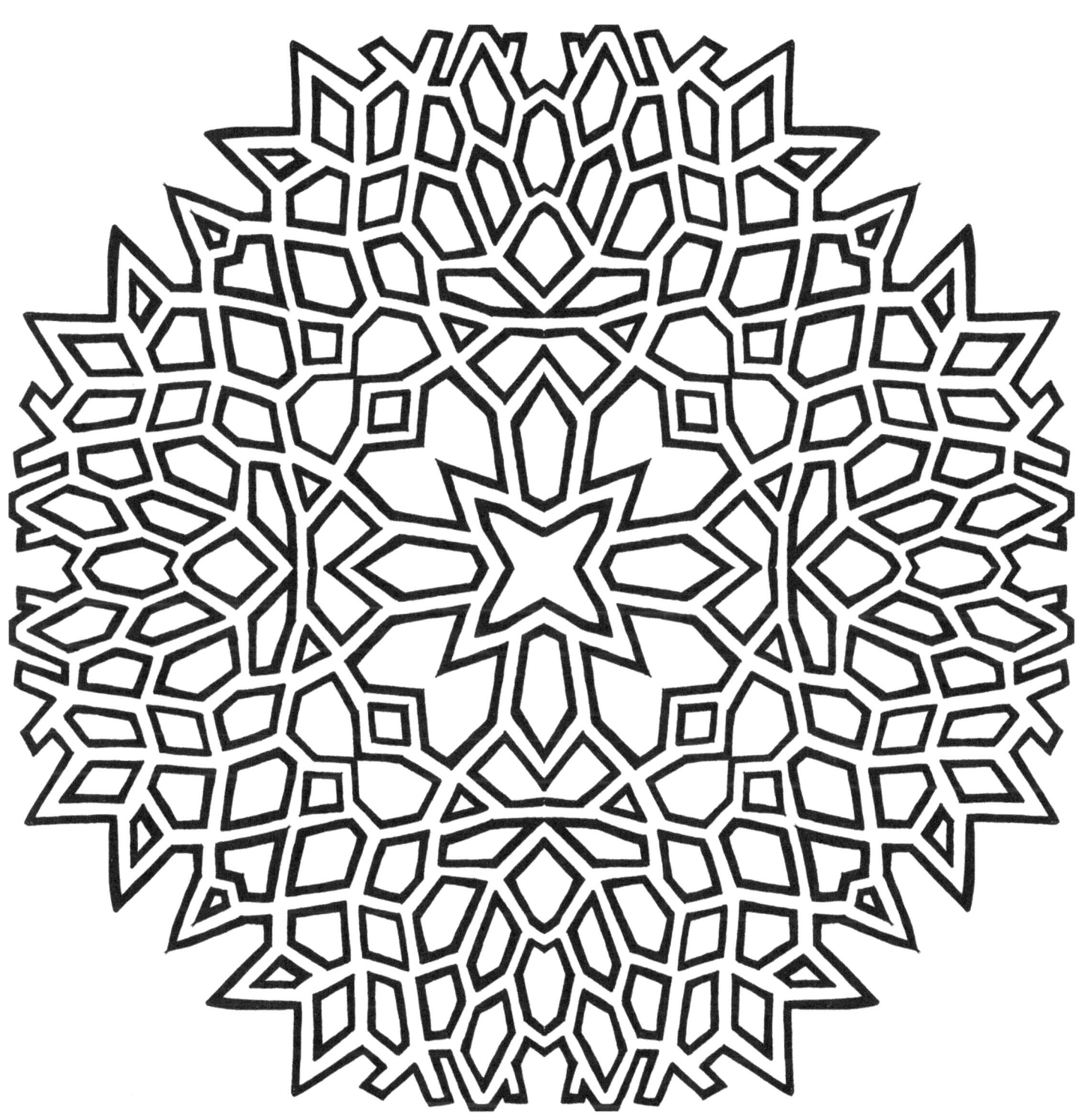

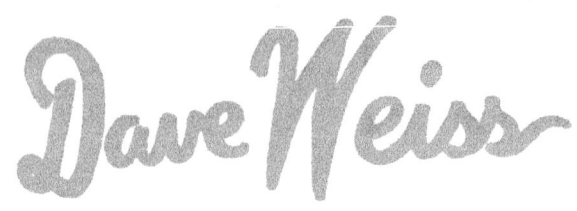

Kaleidoscopics Book 1
"Linear Explosion"

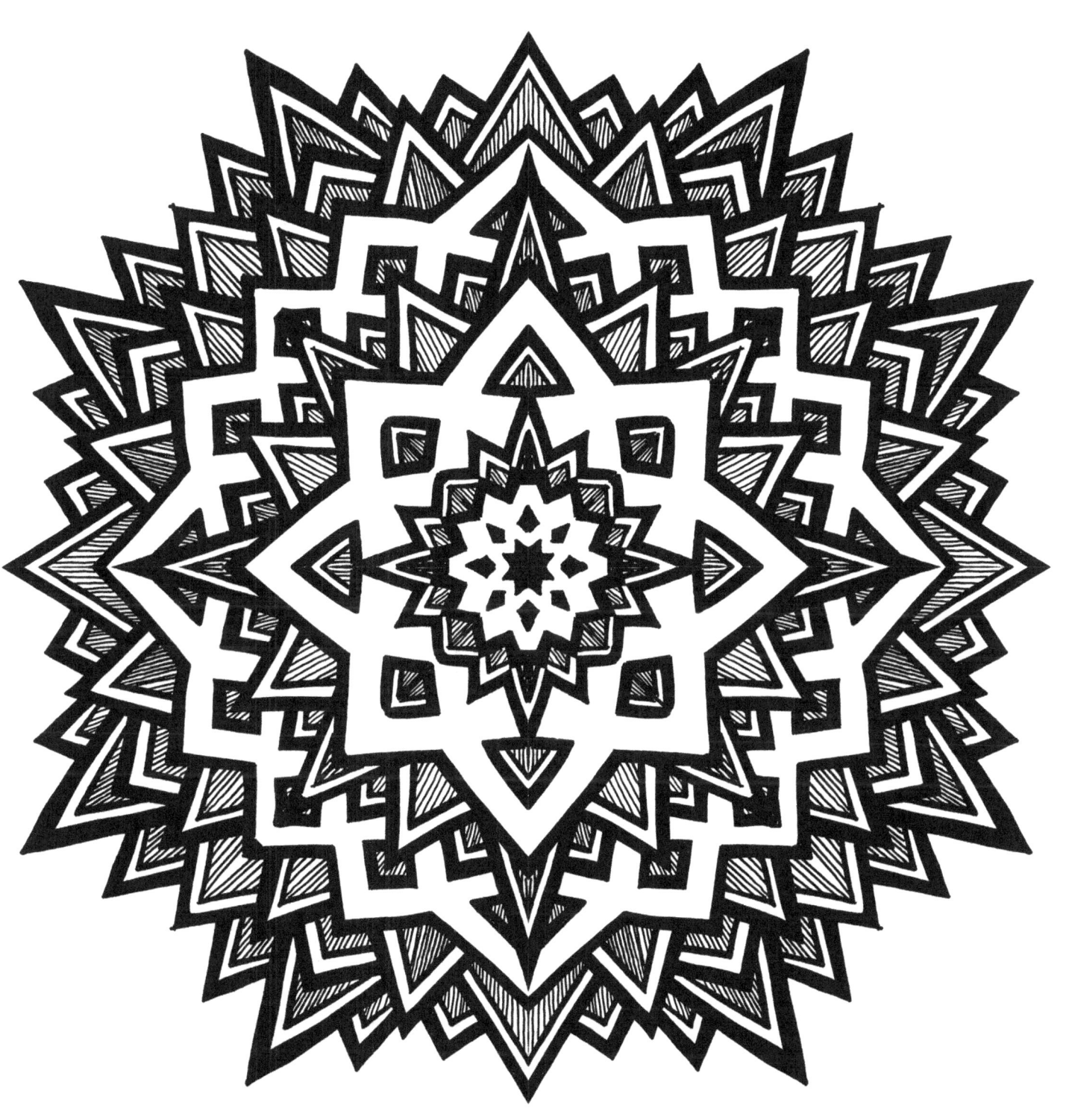

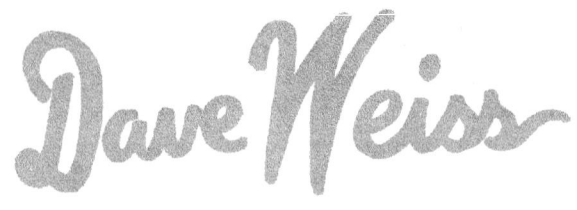

Dave Weiss

Kaleidoscopics Book 1
"Pointed Conversation"

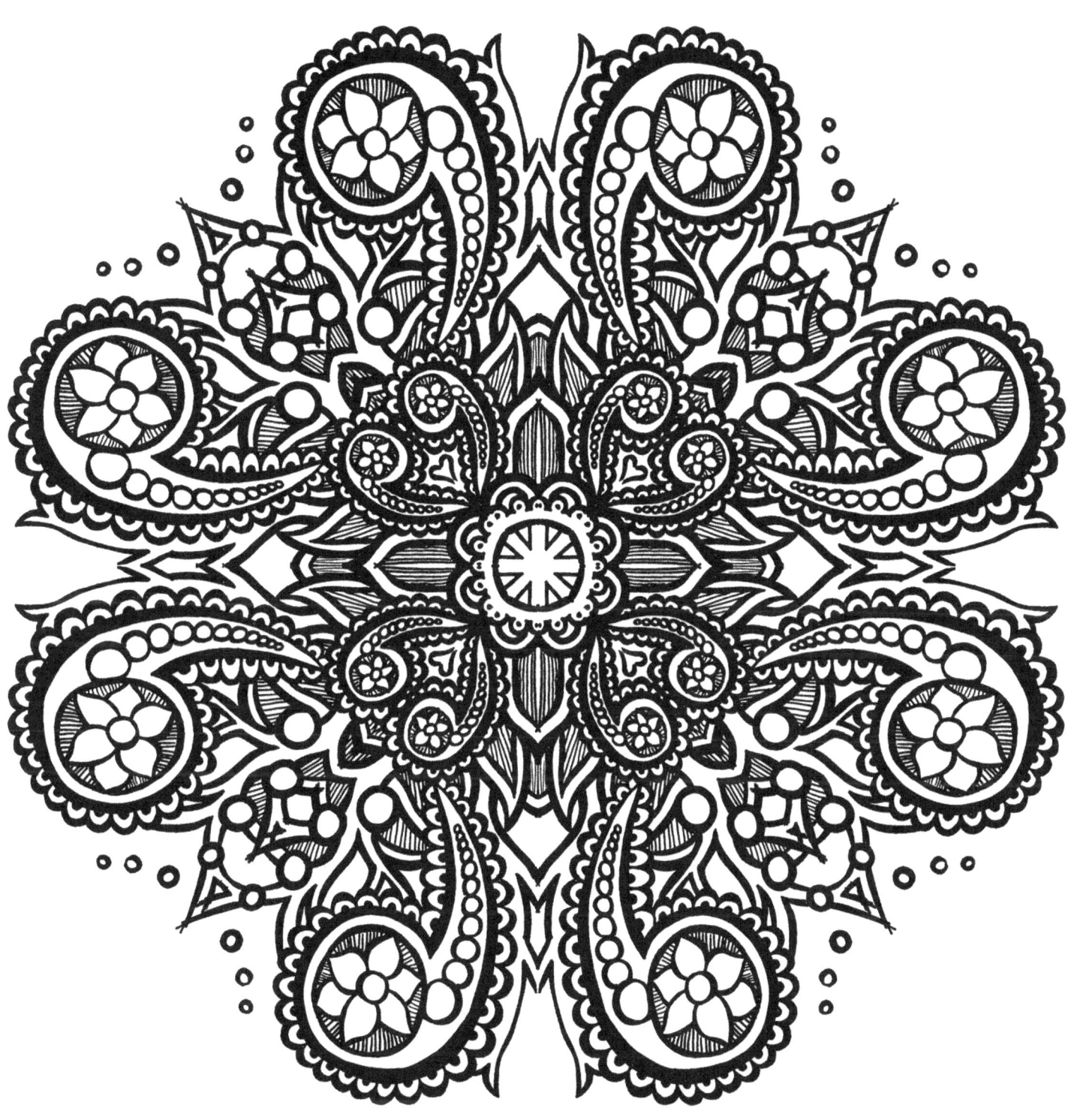

Dave Weiss

Kaleidoscopics Book 1
"Paisley Party"

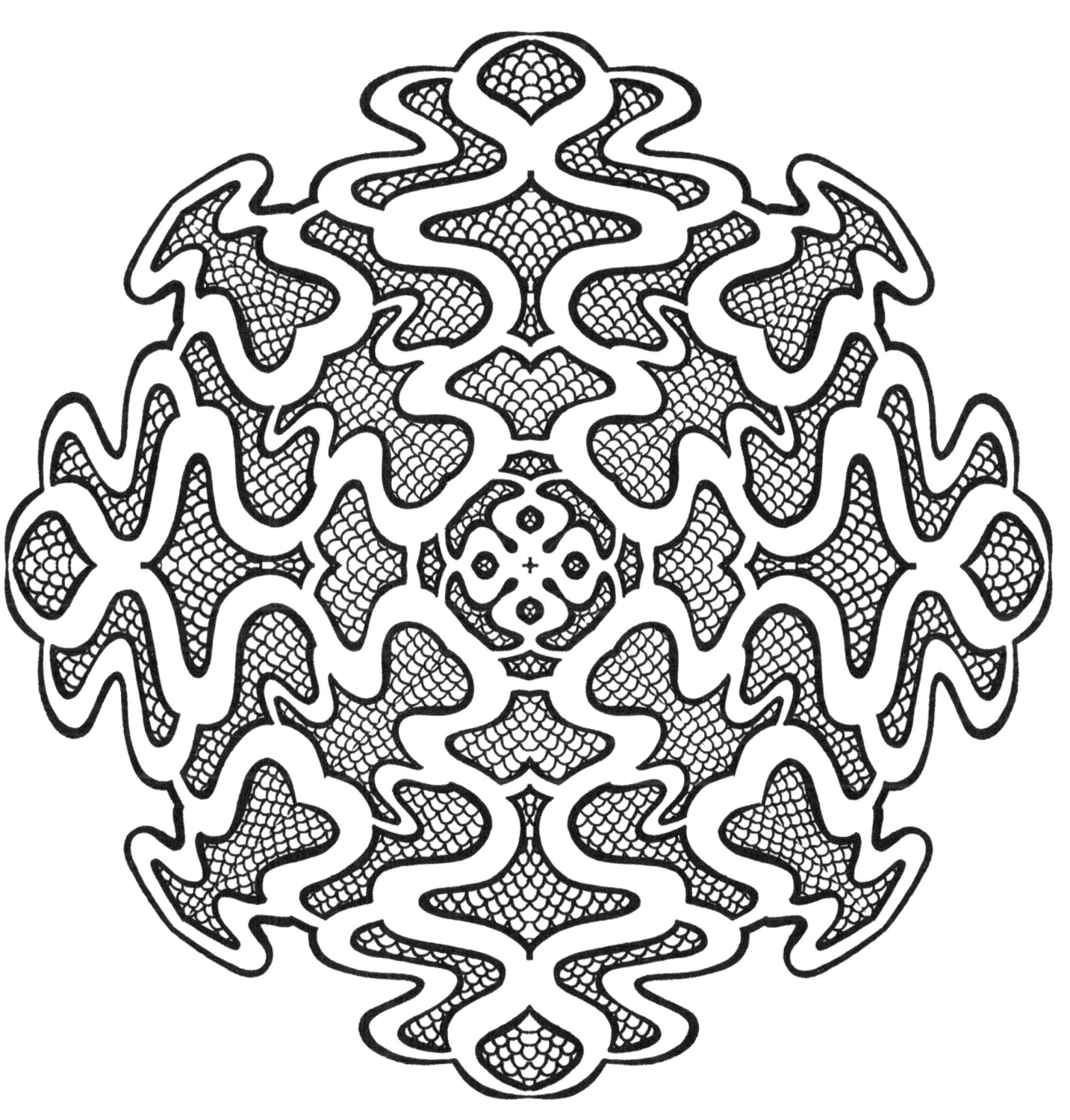

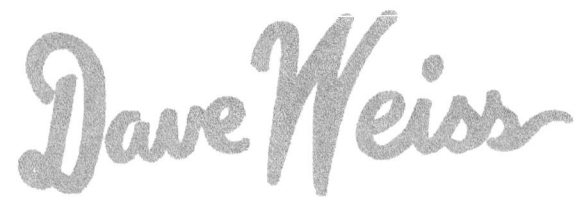

Kaleidoscopics Book 1
"Long Winding Path"

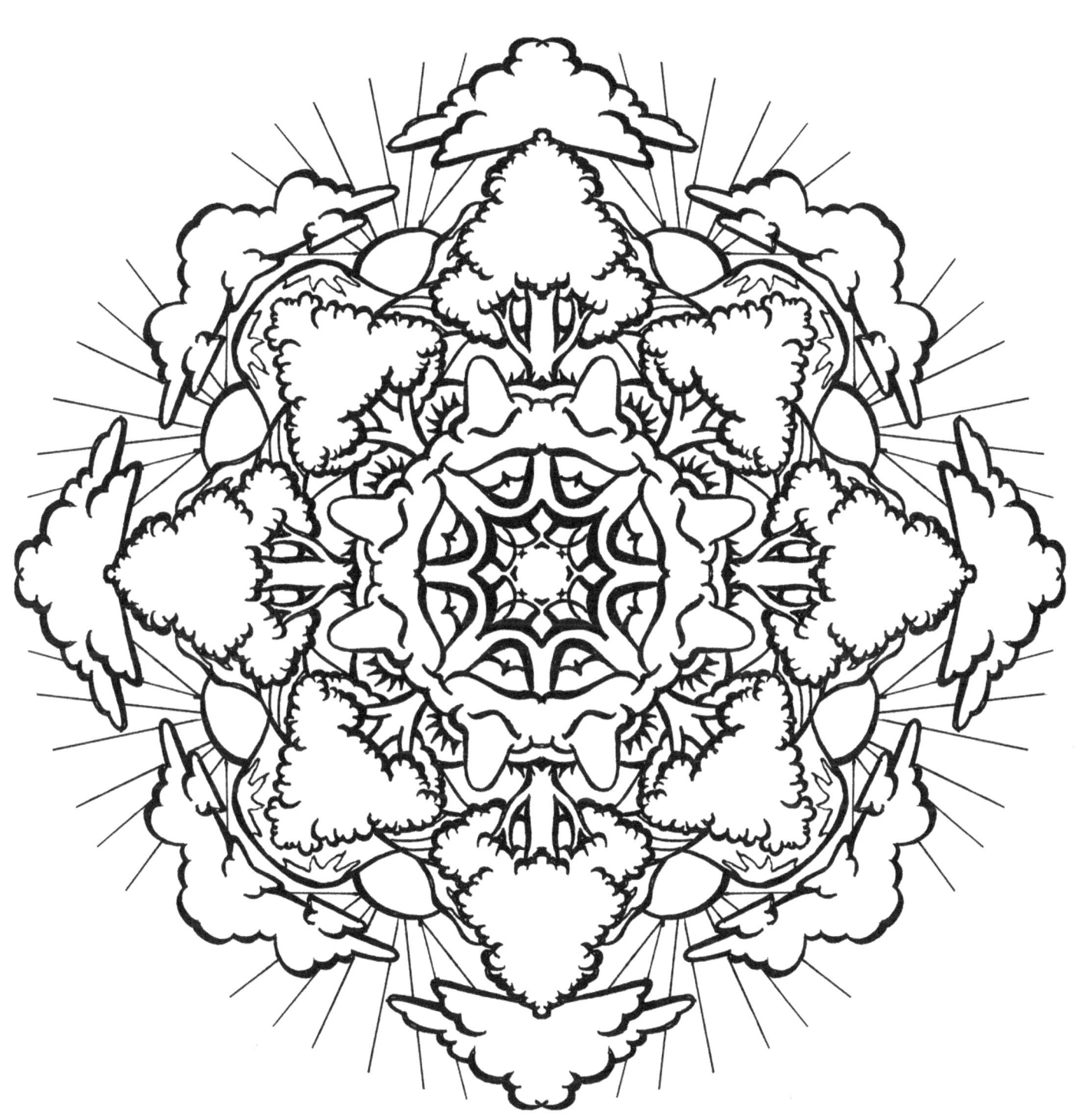

Dave Weiss

Kaleidoscopics Book 1
"Peace and Joy"

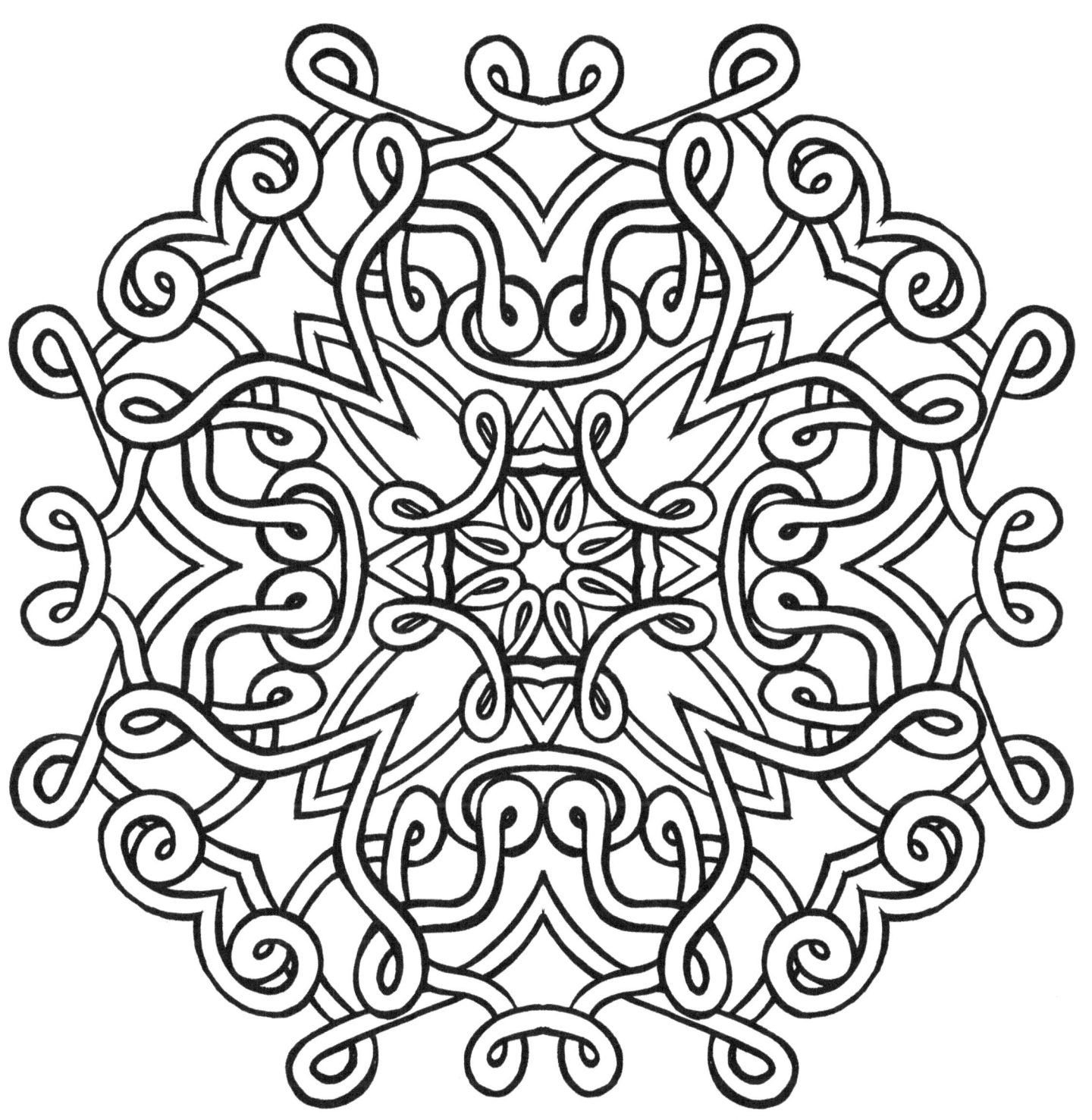

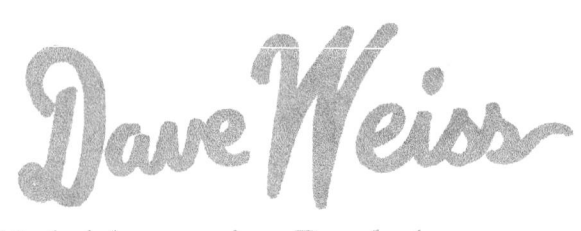

Kaleidoscopics Book 1
"Swirlin' Dervish"

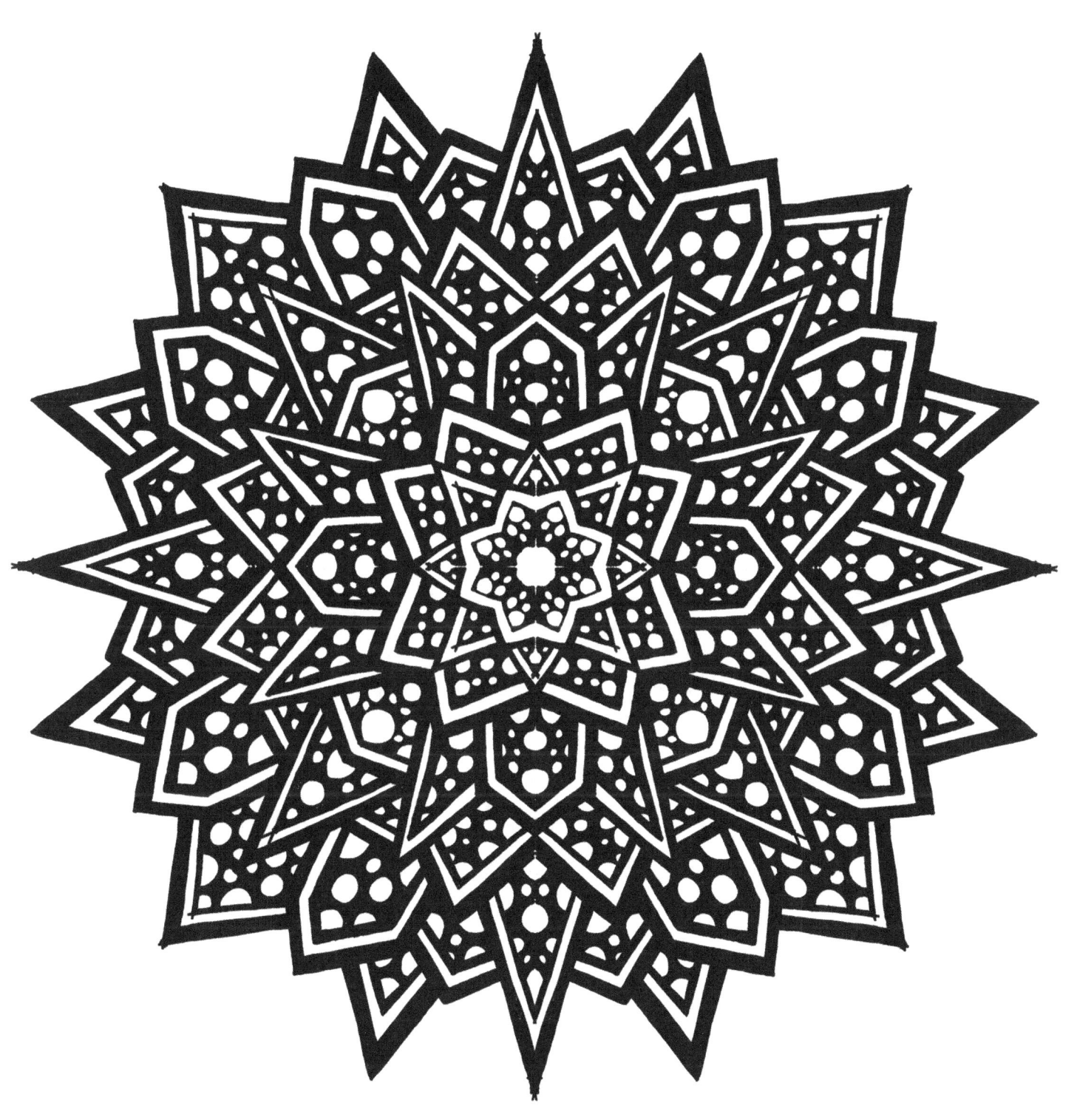

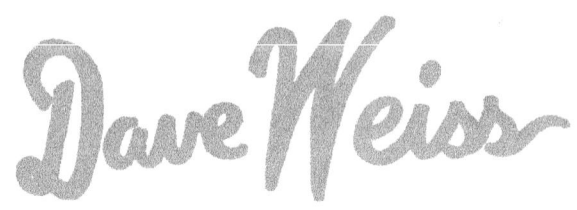

Kaleidoscopics Book 1
"Dark Crystal"

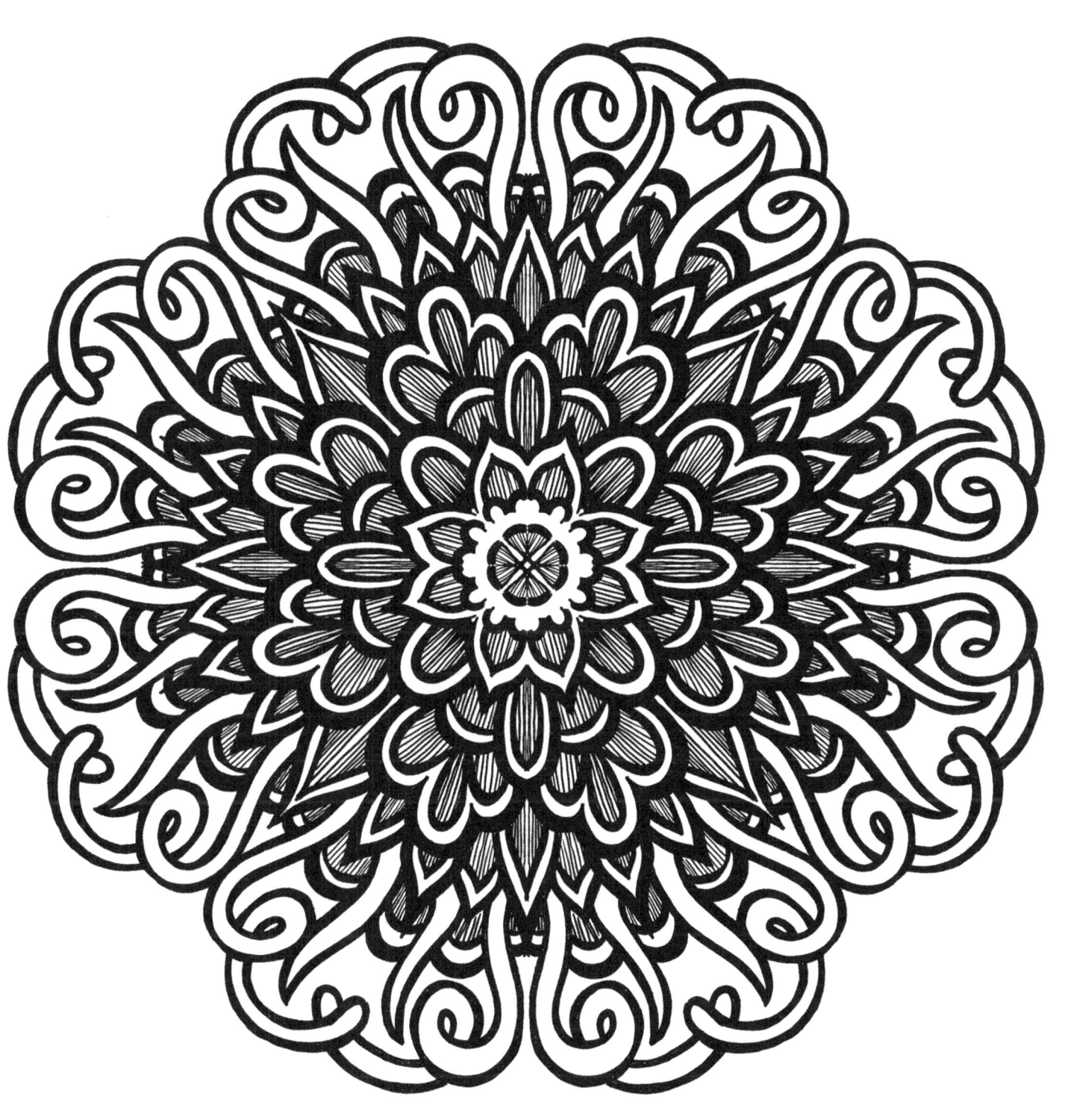

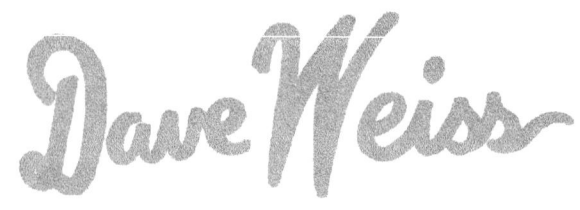

Dave Weiss

Kaleidoscopics Book 1
"Petals and Tendrils"

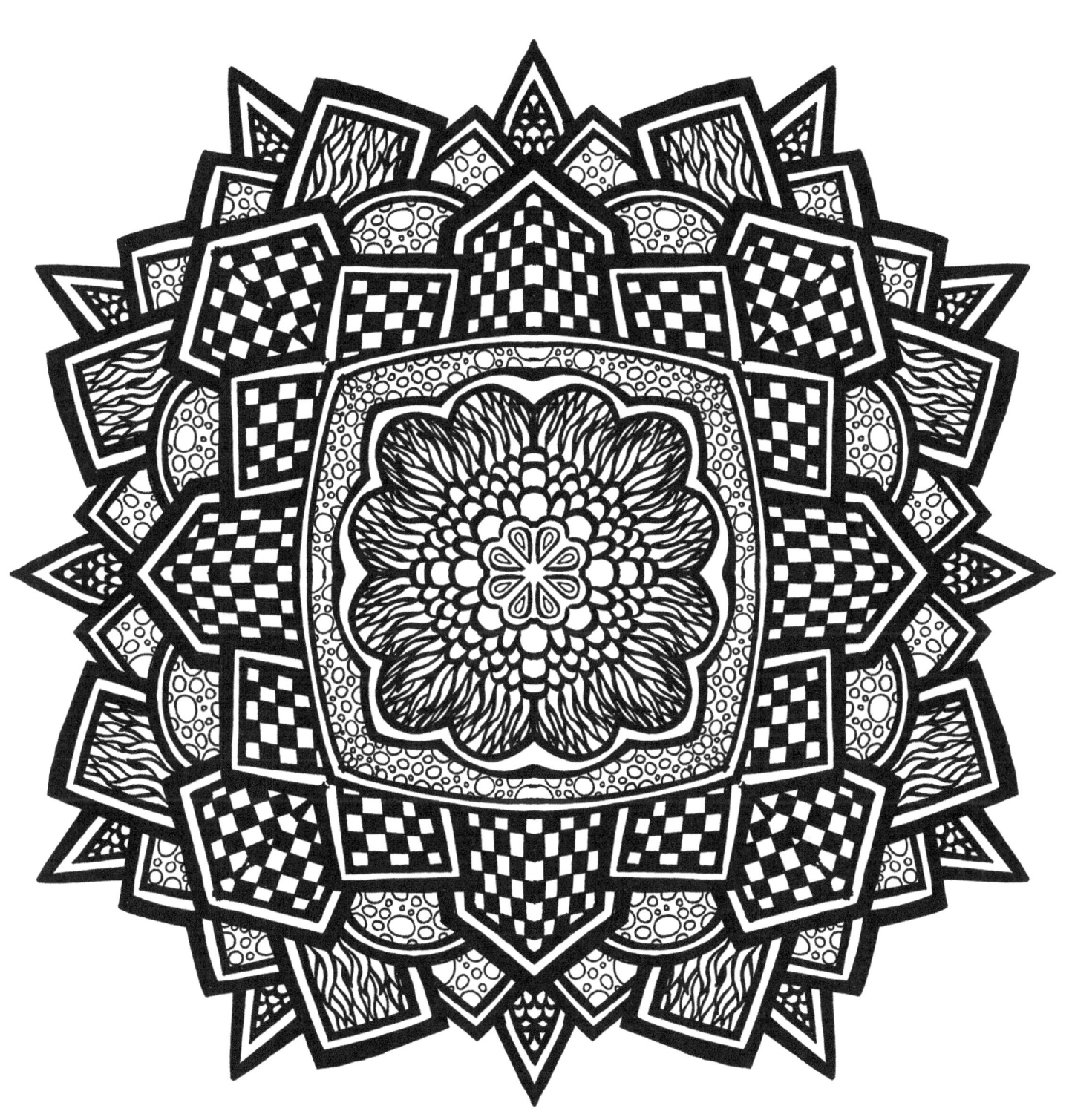

Dave Weiss

Kaleidoscopics Book 1
"Tower Flower (from above)"

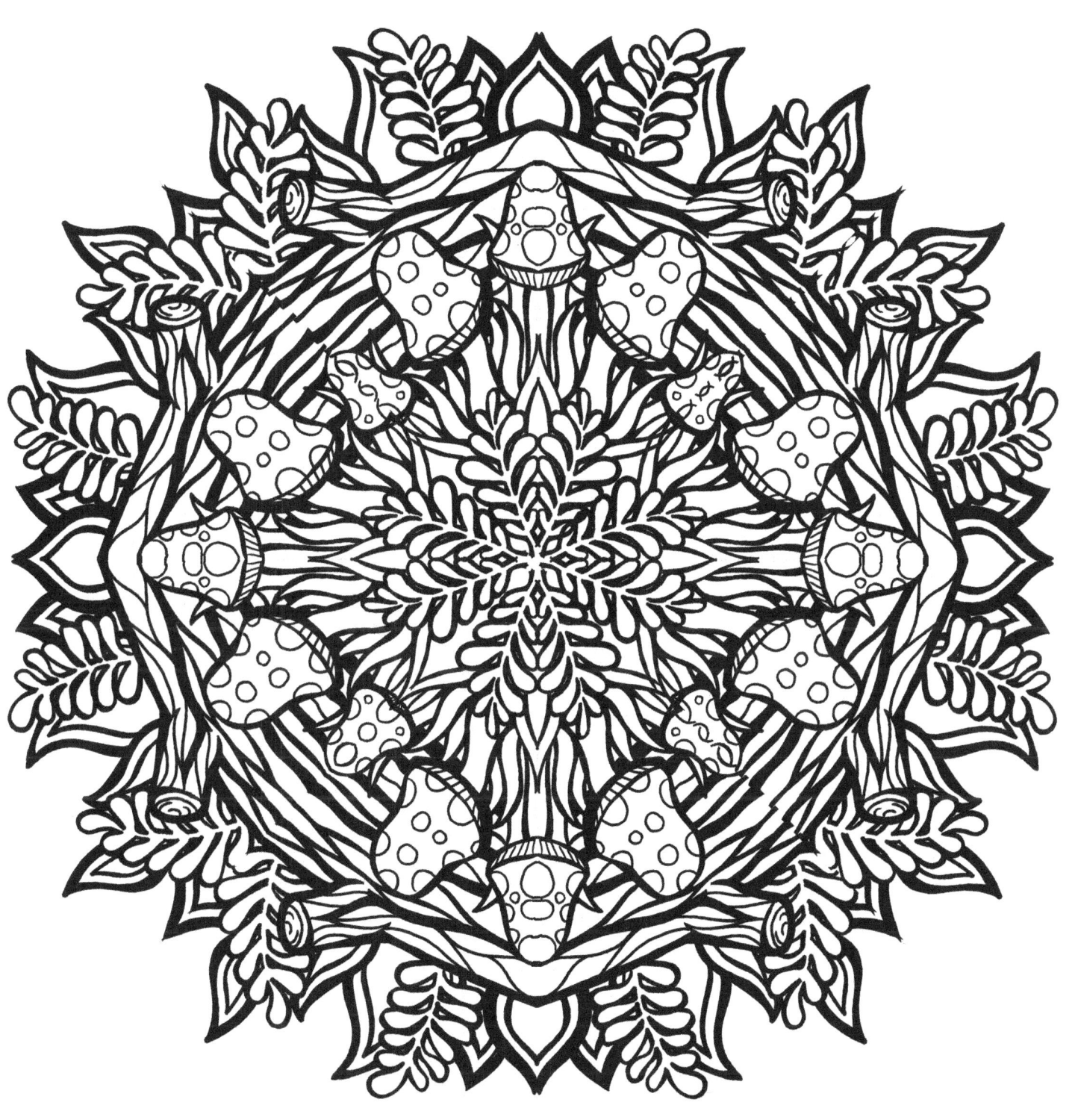

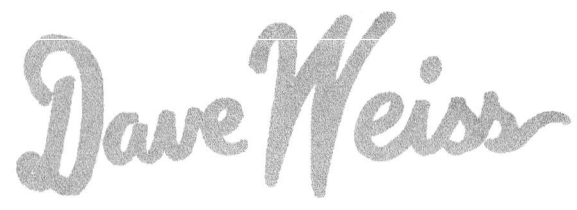

Kaleidoscopics Book 1
"Forest Floor"

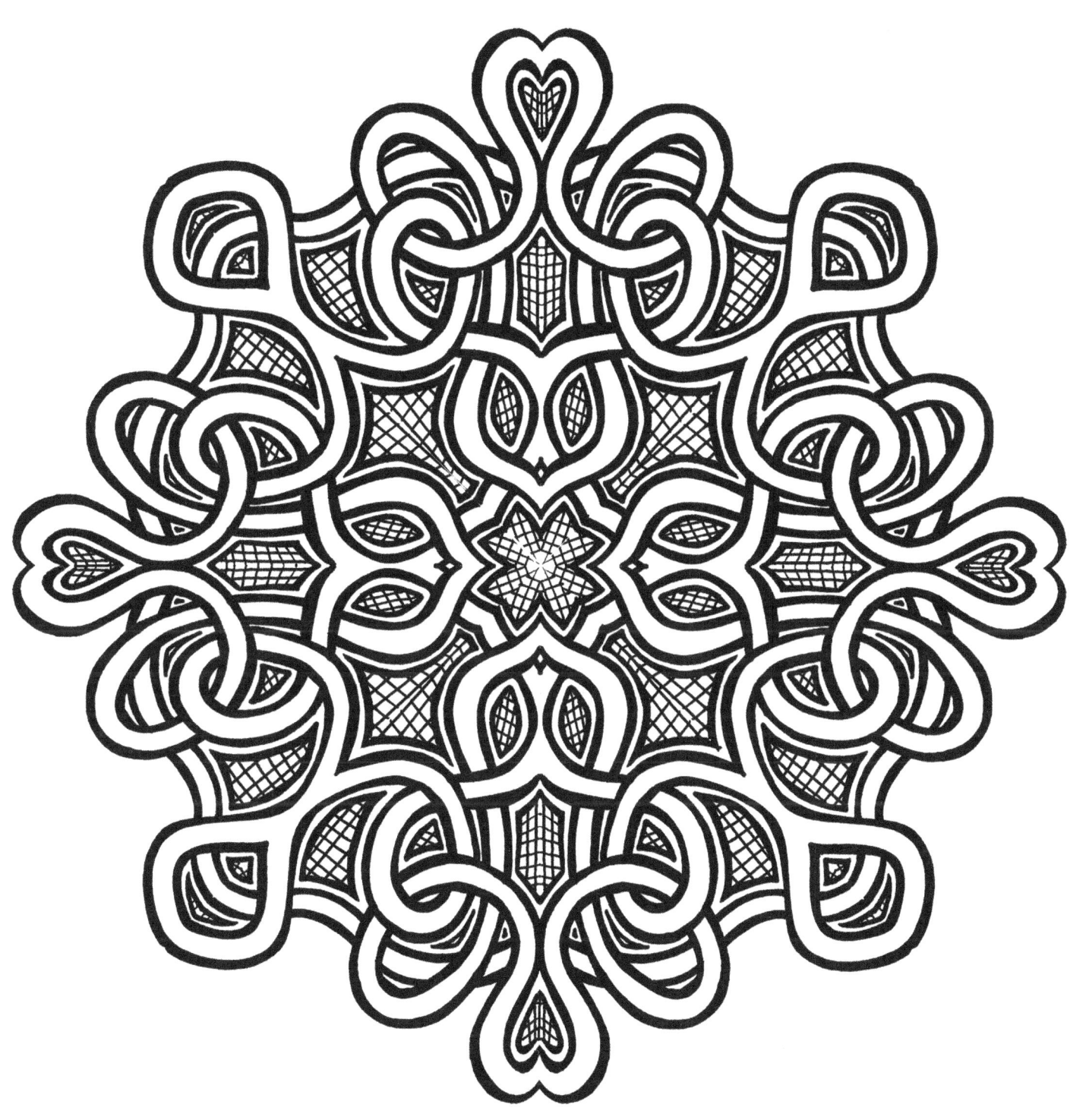

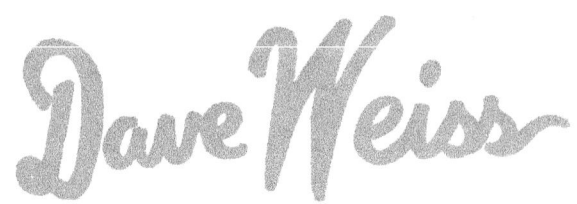

Kaleidoscopics Book 1
"Interconnected"

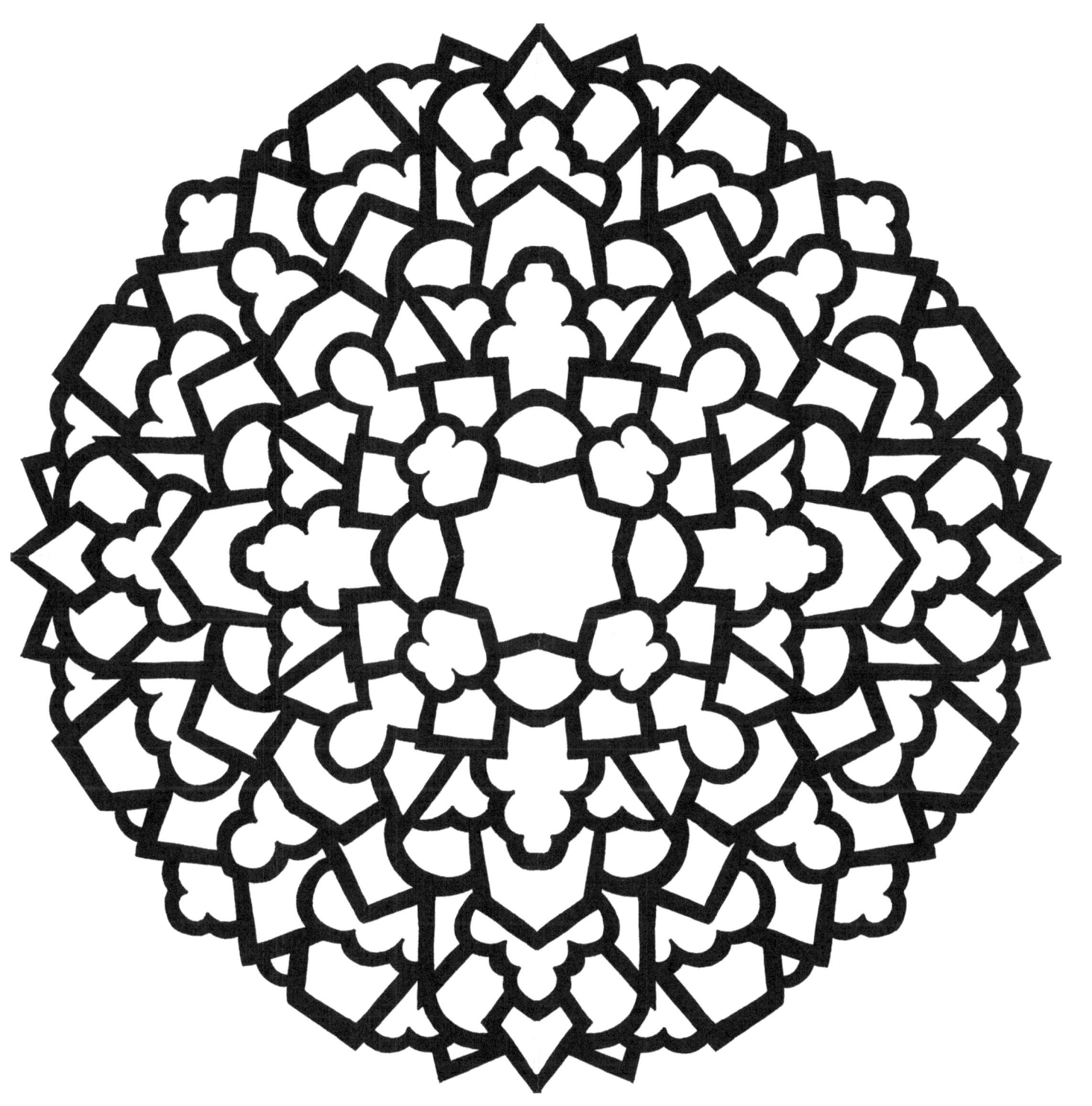

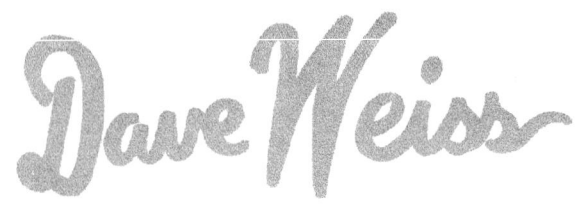

Kaleidoscopics Book 1
"Shapes and Forms"

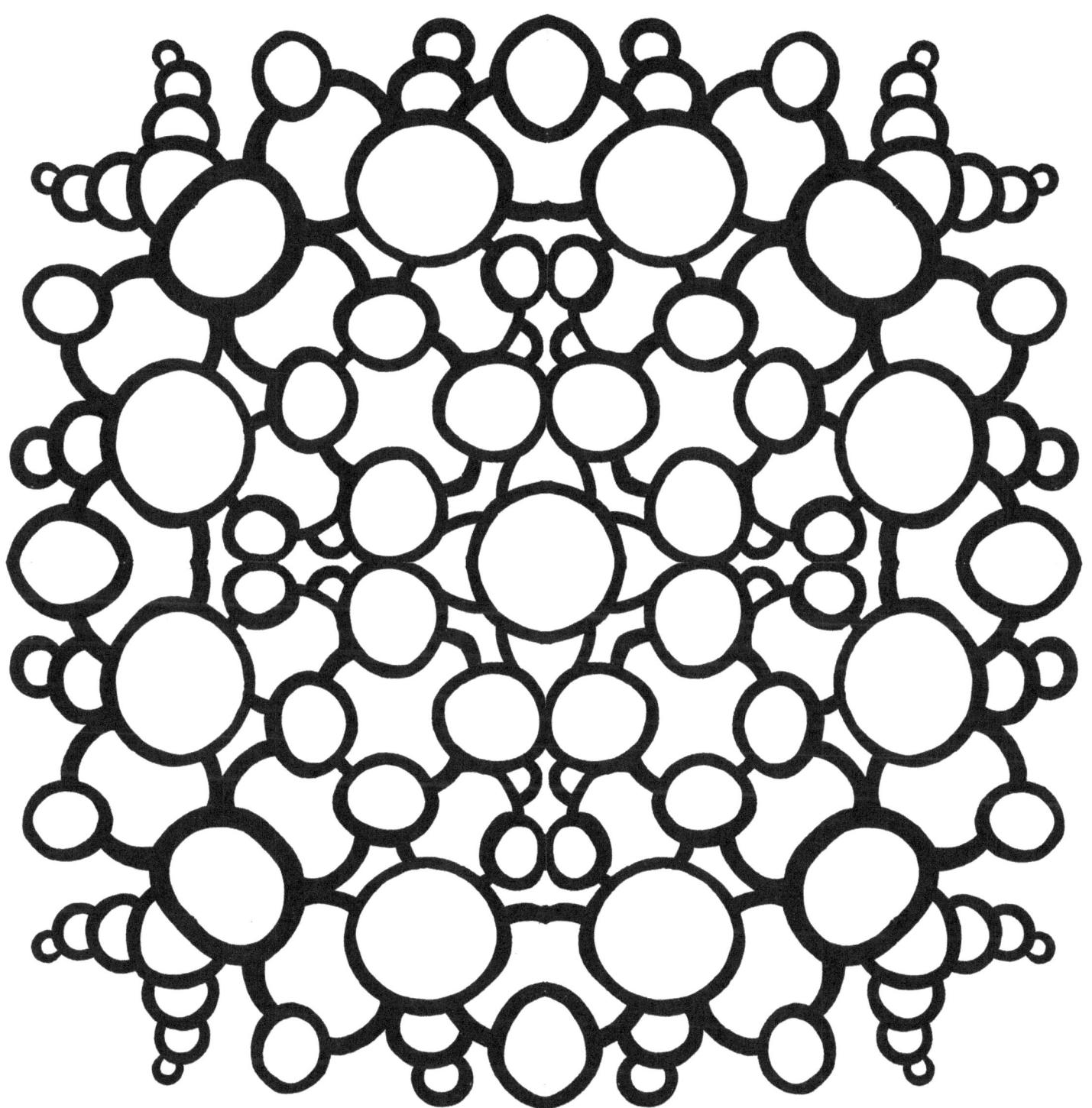

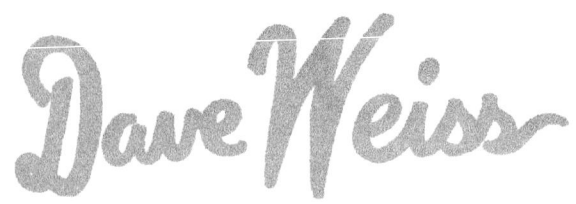

Dave Weiss

Kaleidoscopics Book 1
"Molecular Level"

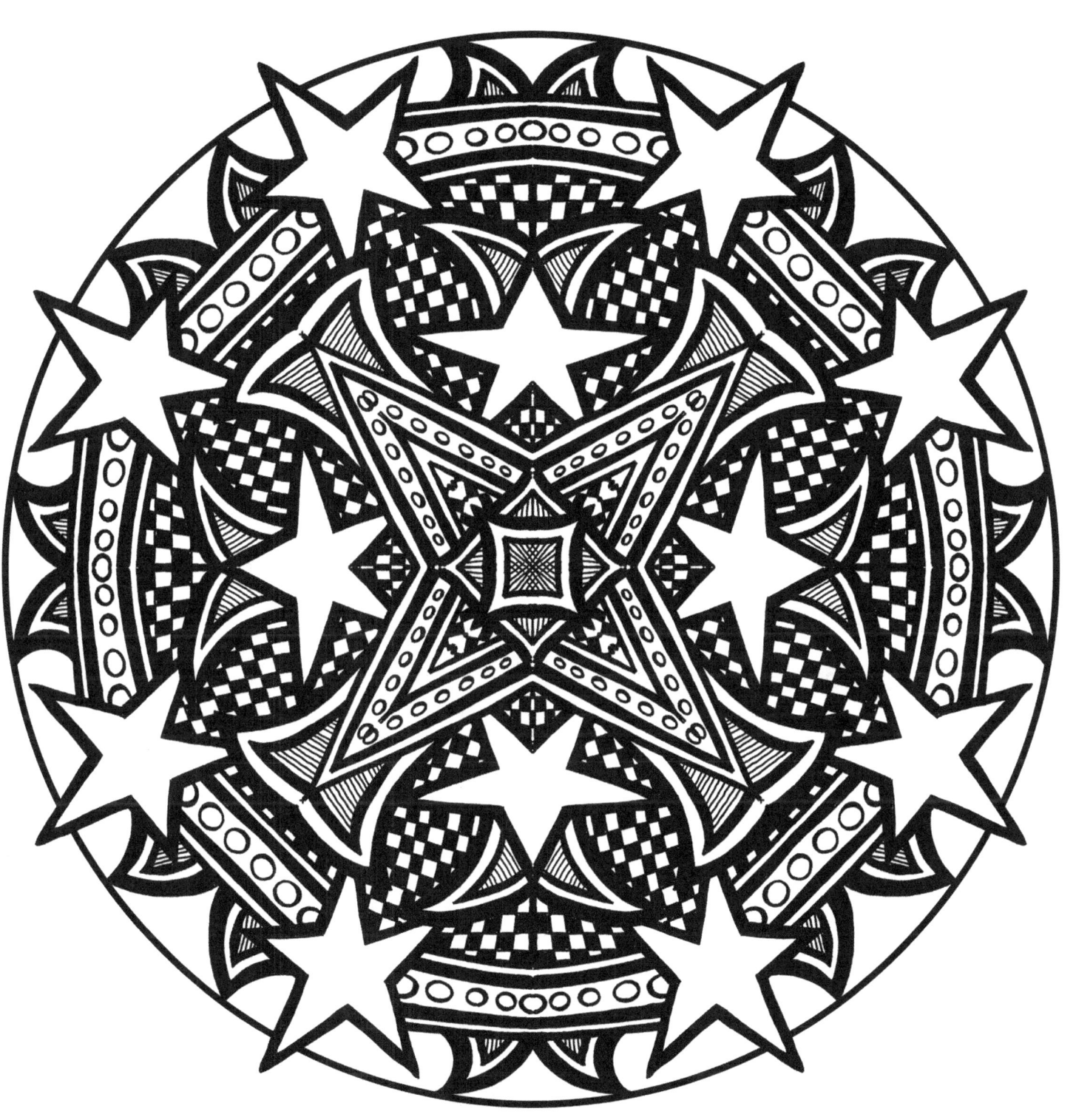

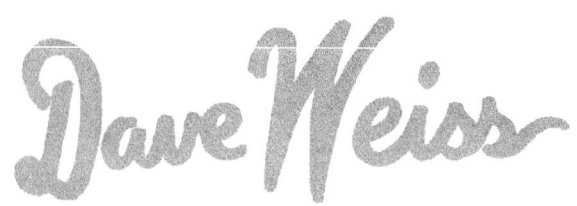

Kaleidoscopics Book 1
"Star-board"

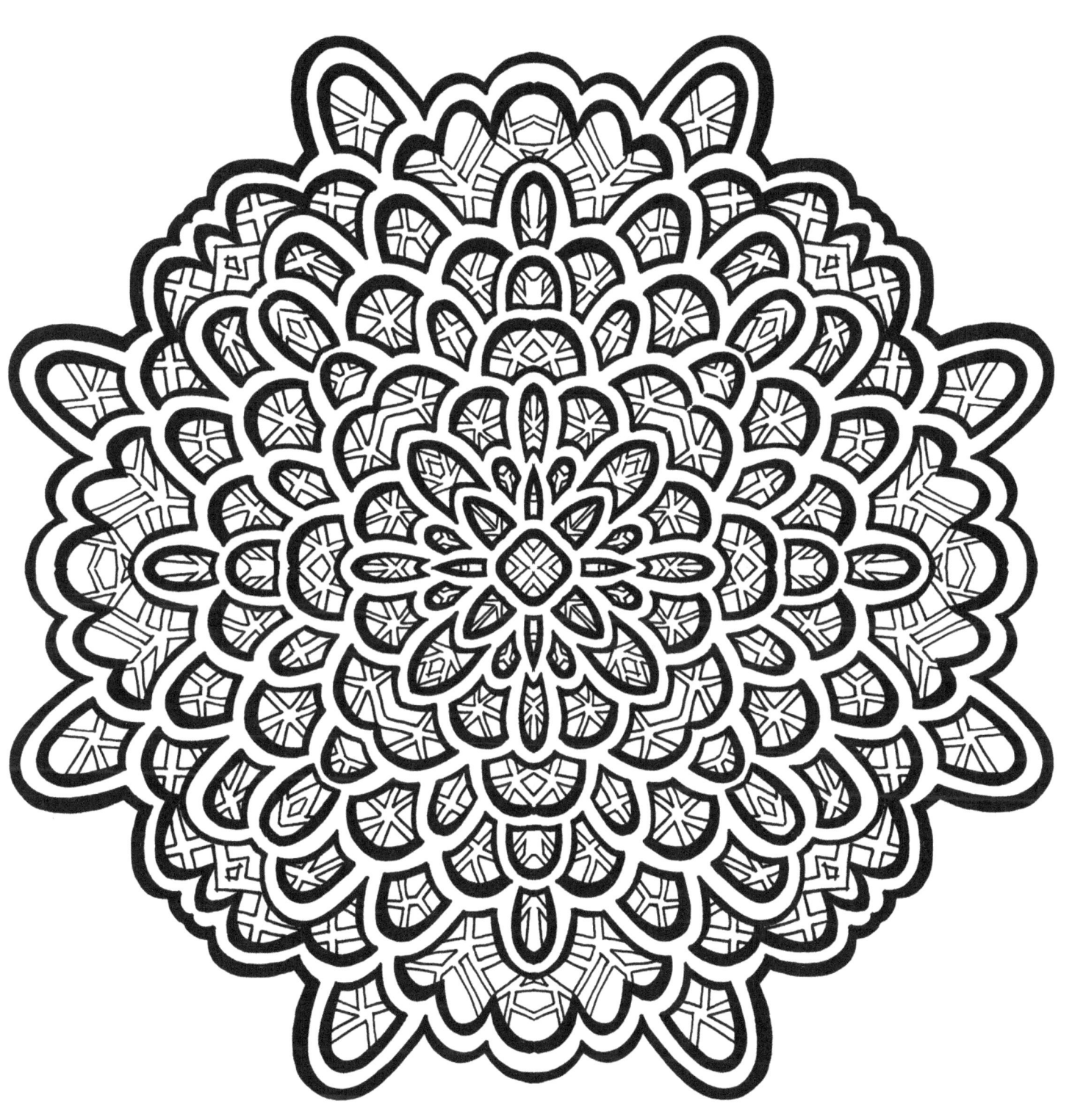

Dave Weiss

Kaleidoscopics Book 1
"Curves and Lines"

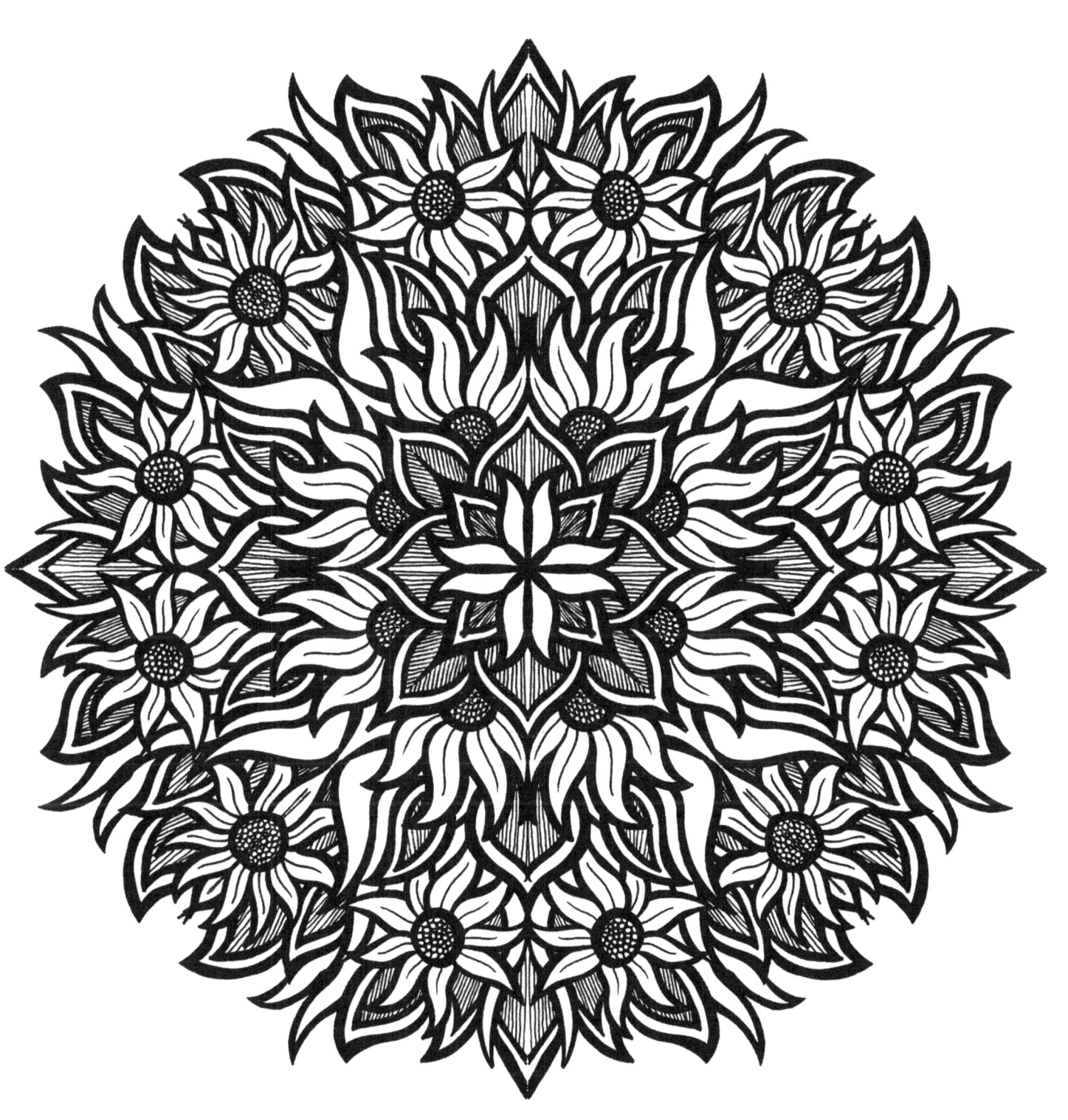

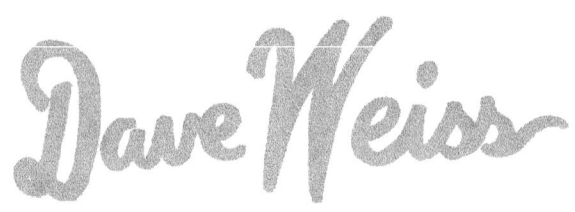

Kaleidoscopics Book 1
"Daisies"

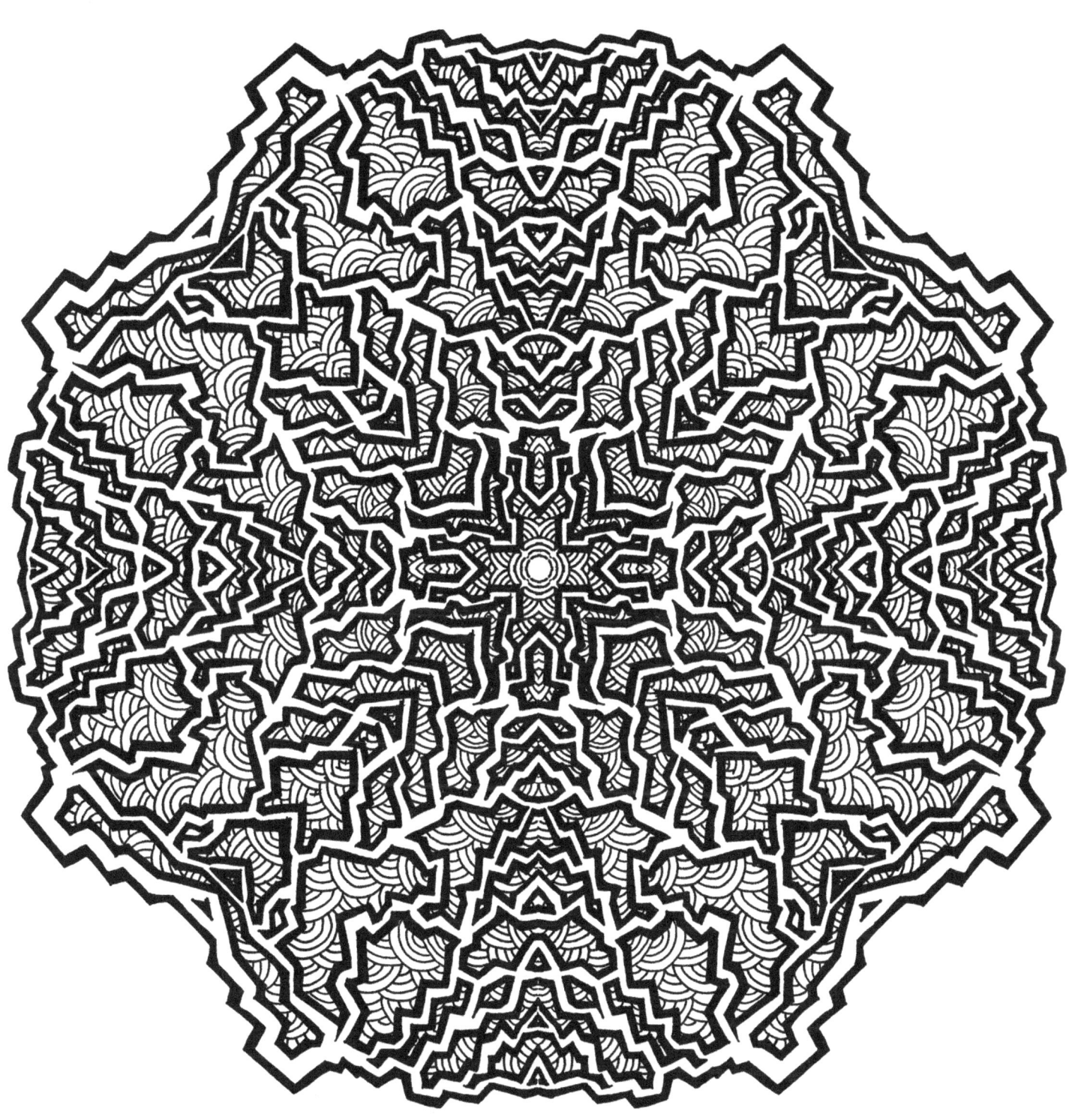

Dave Weiss

Kaleidoscopics Book 1
"Rainbow in the Dark"

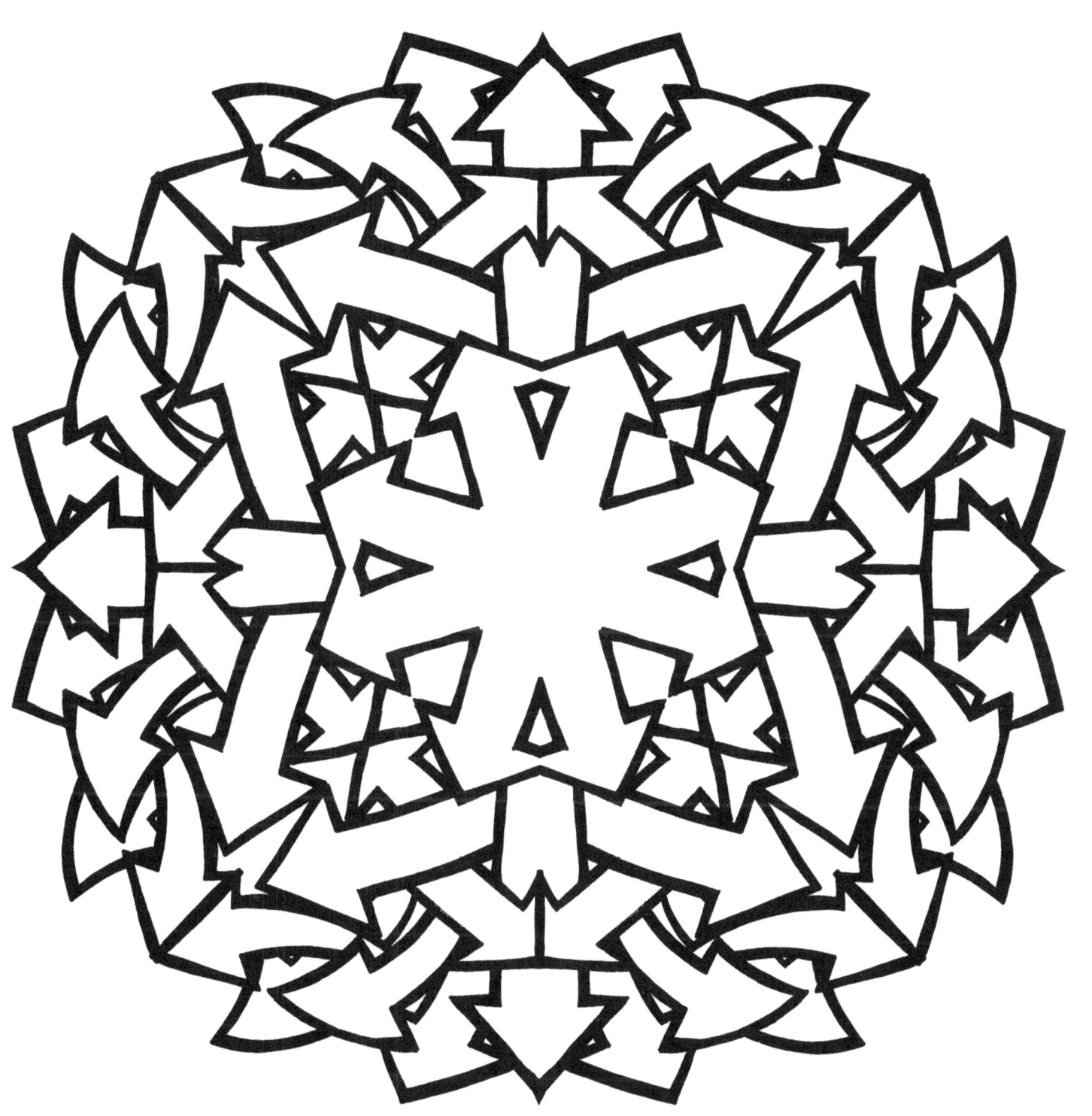

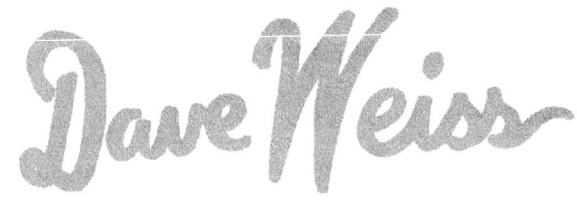

Kaleidoscopics Book 1
"Which Way Is Up?"

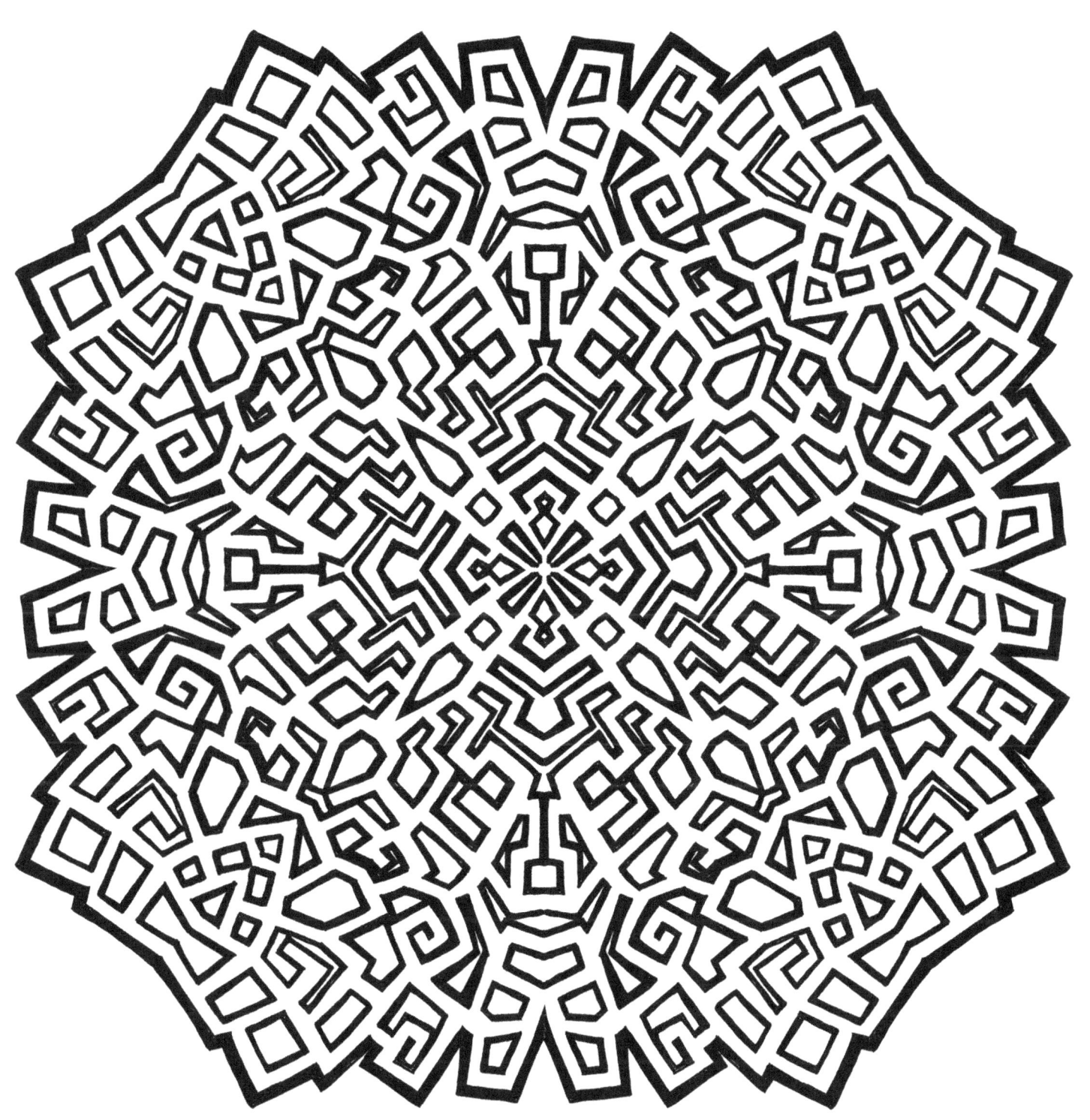

Dave Weiss

Kaleidoscopics Book 1
"Ah-Maze-Zing"

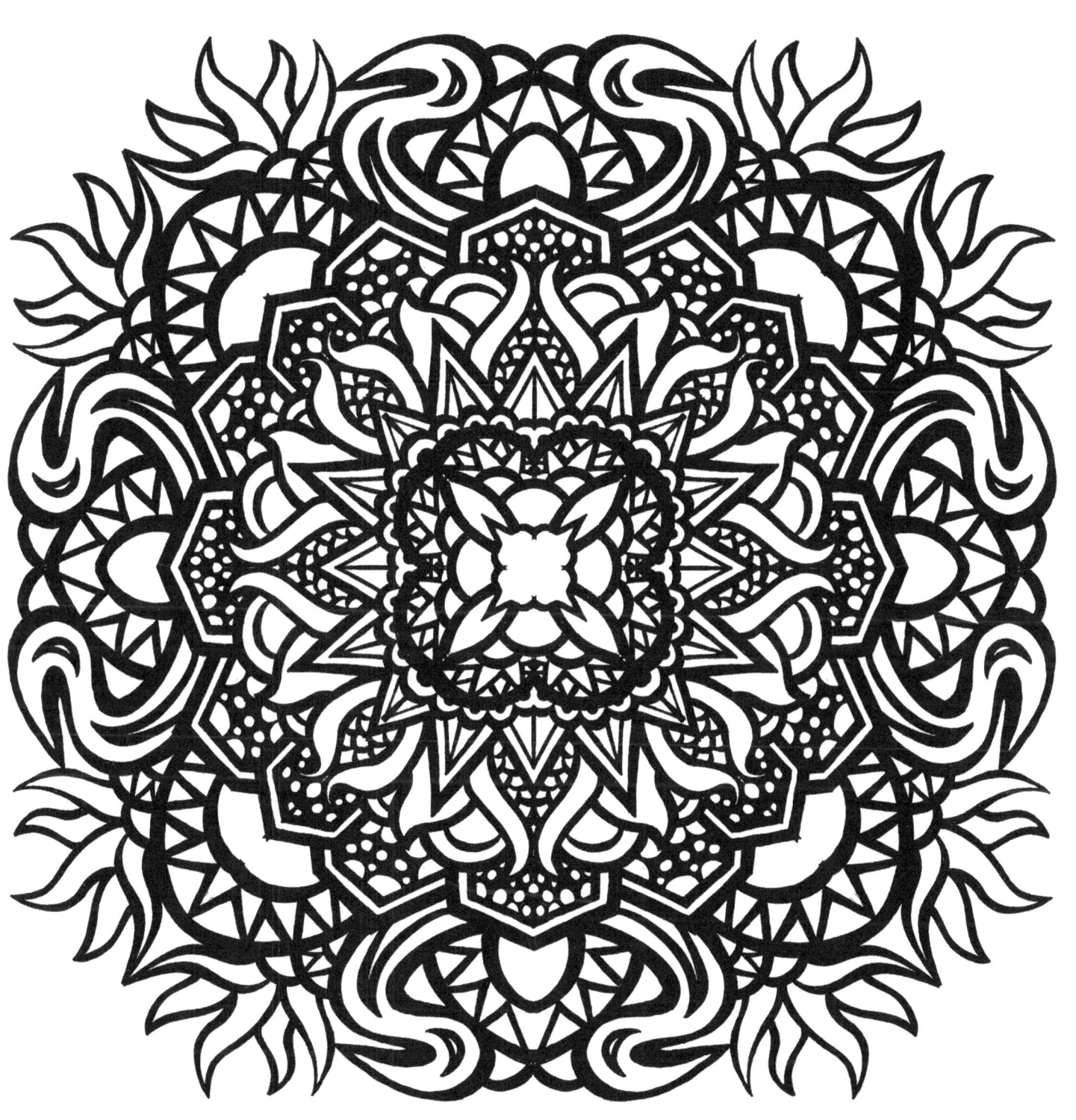

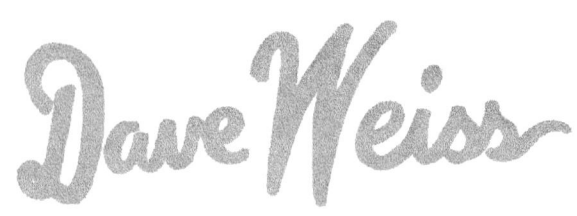
Kaleidoscopics Book 1
"Phantasia"

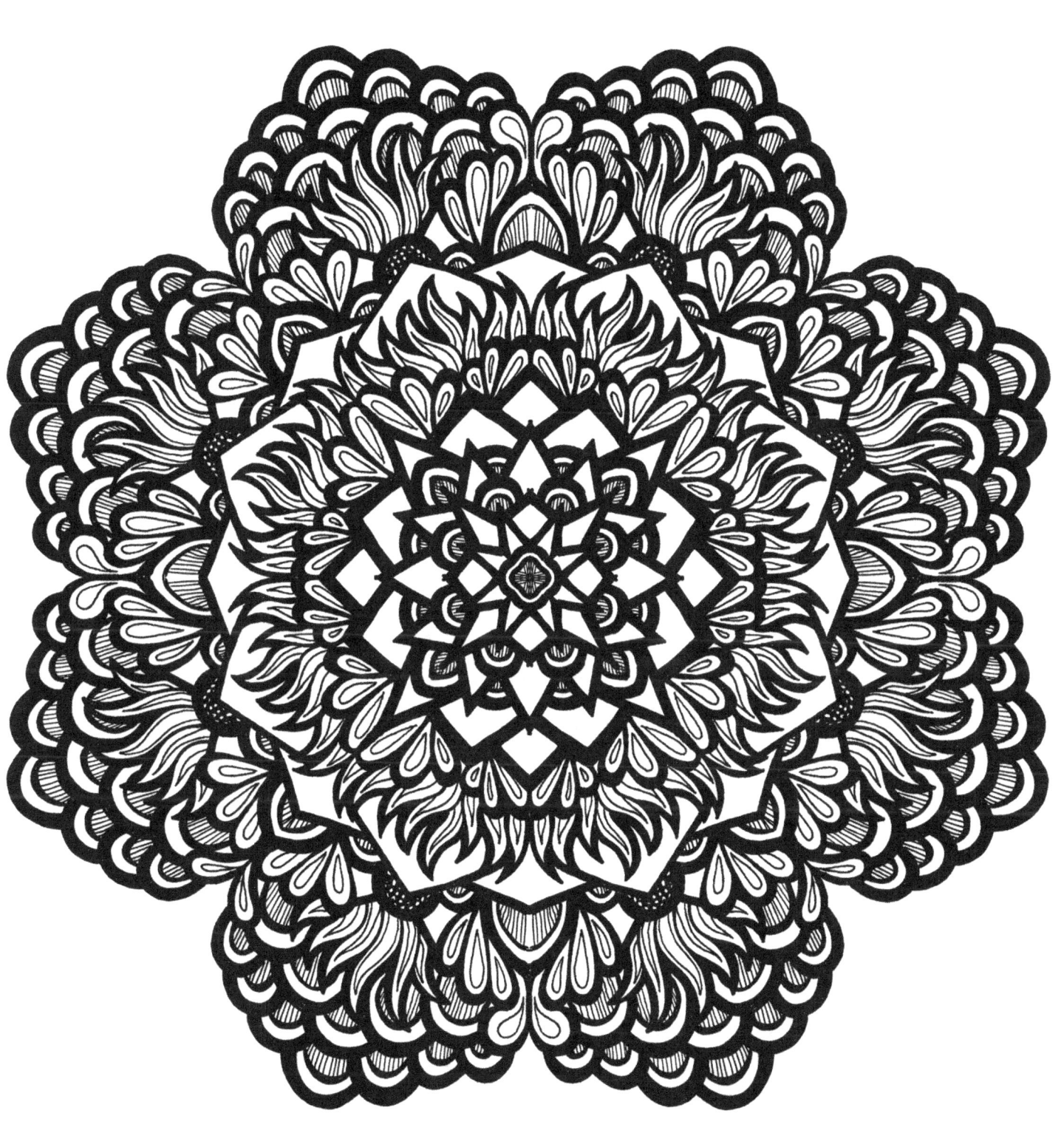

Dave Weiss

Kaleidoscopics Book 1
"Abstraction Distraction"

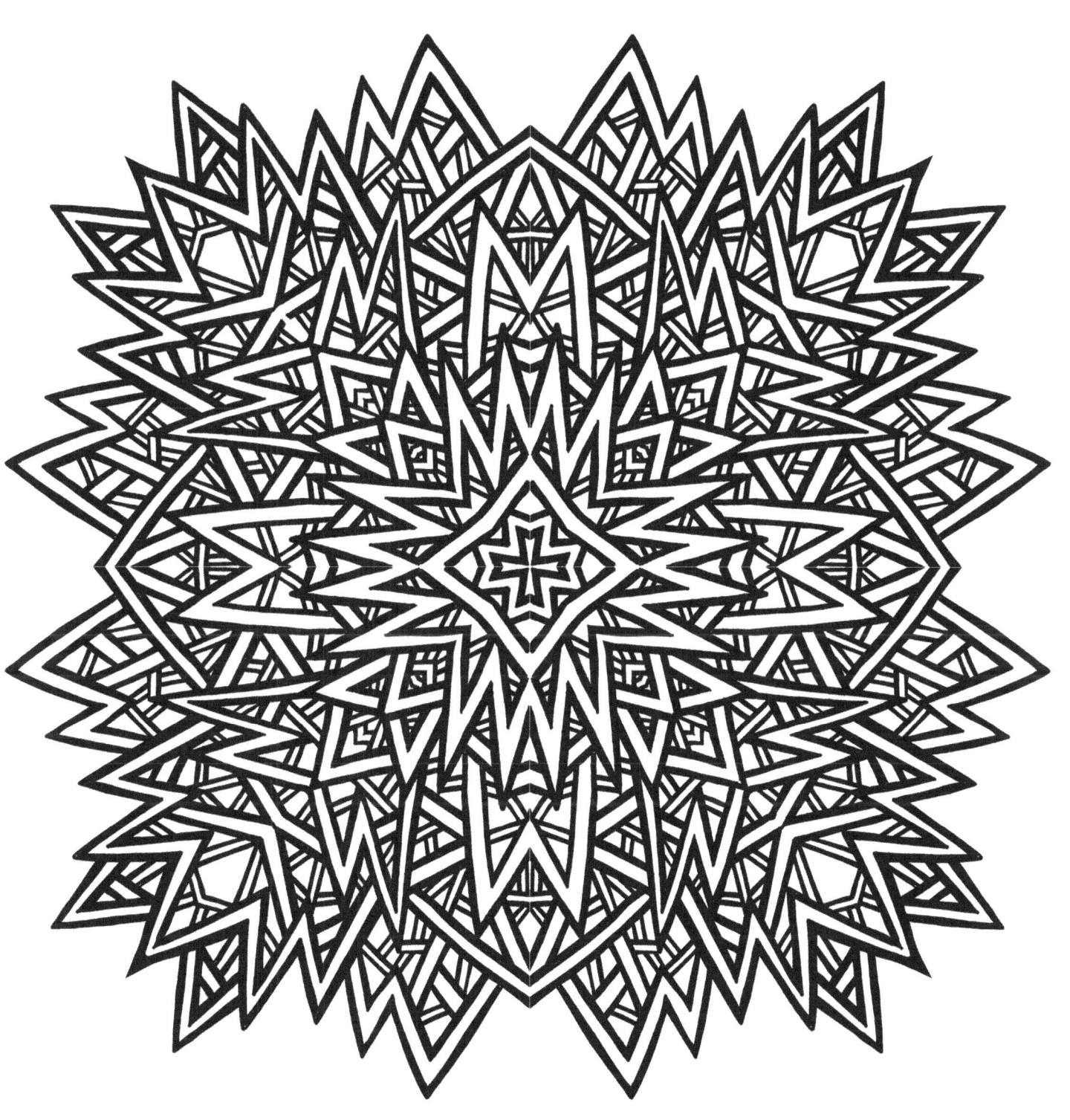

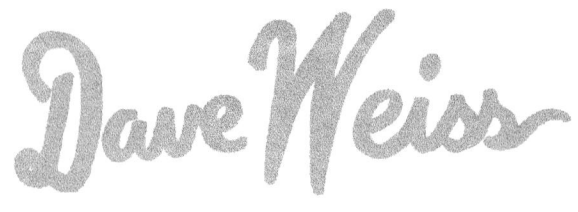

Kaleidoscopics Book 1
"Angular Masses"

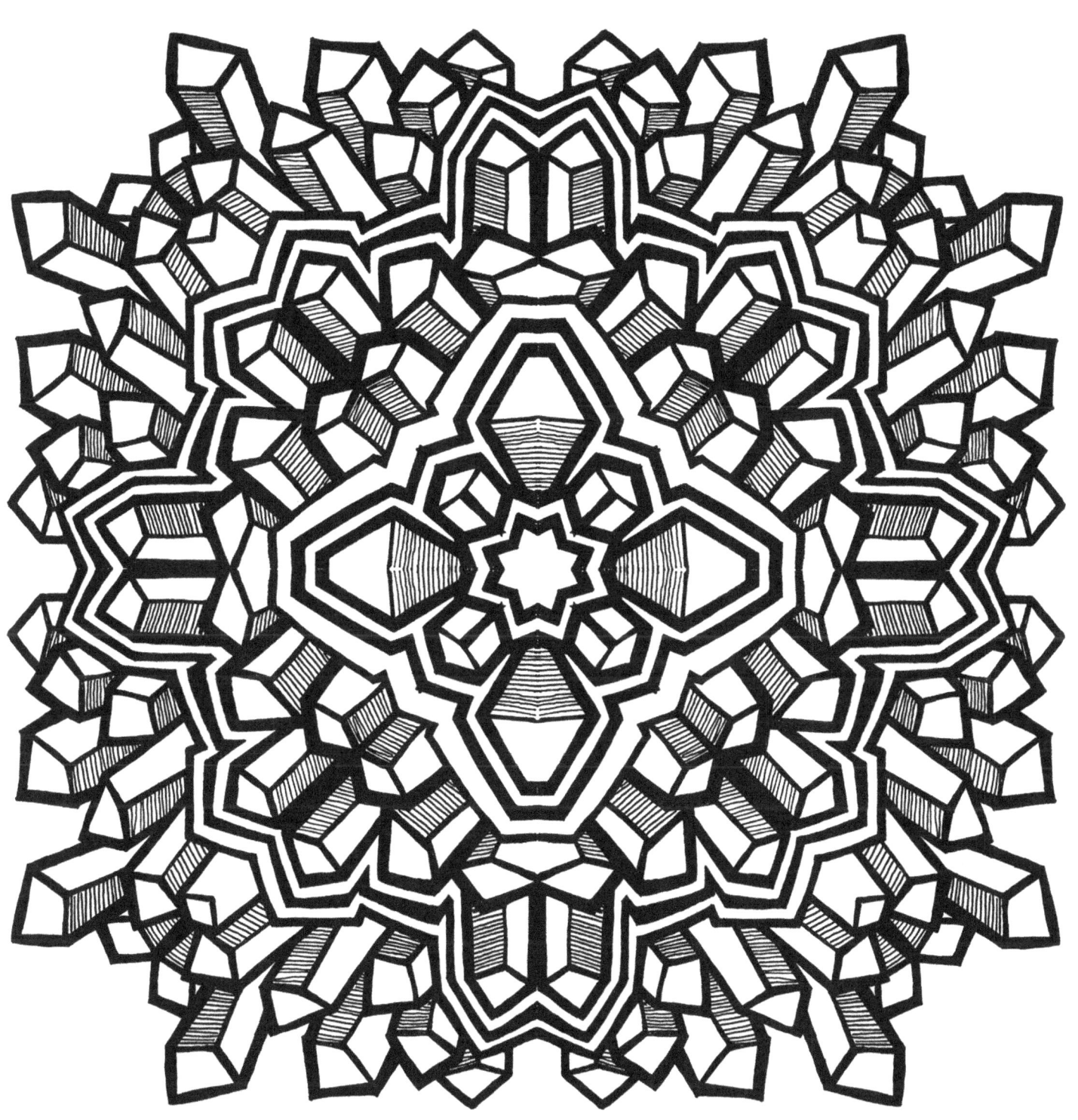

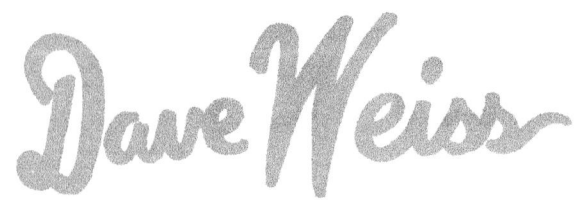

Kaleidoscopics Book 1
"Geodesic"

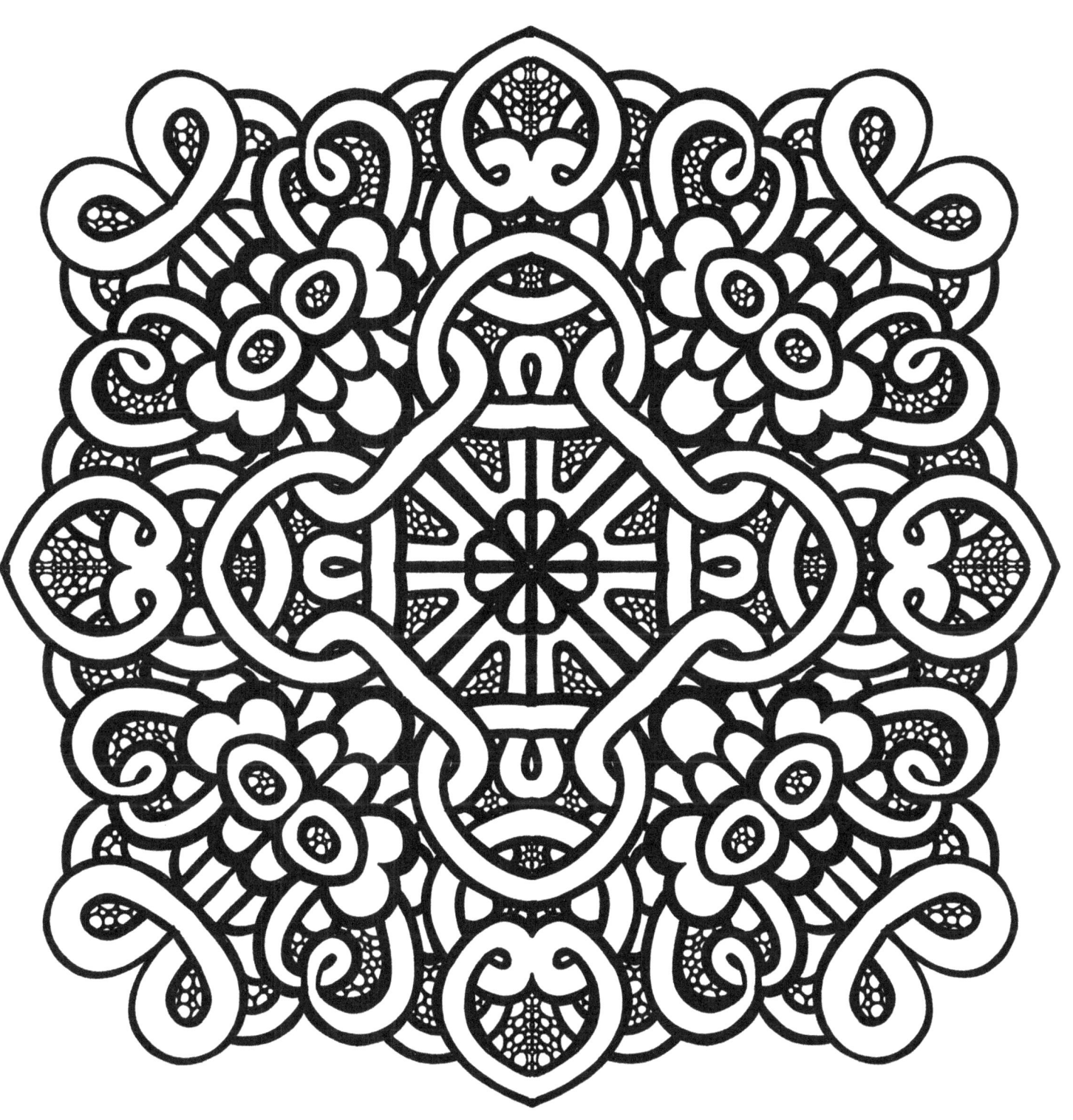

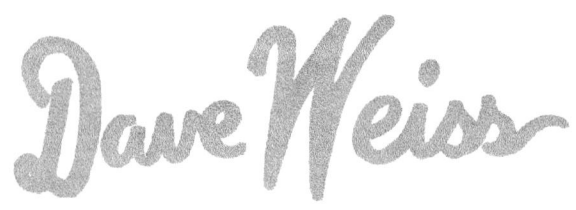

Kaleidoscopics Book 1
"Unity Loop"

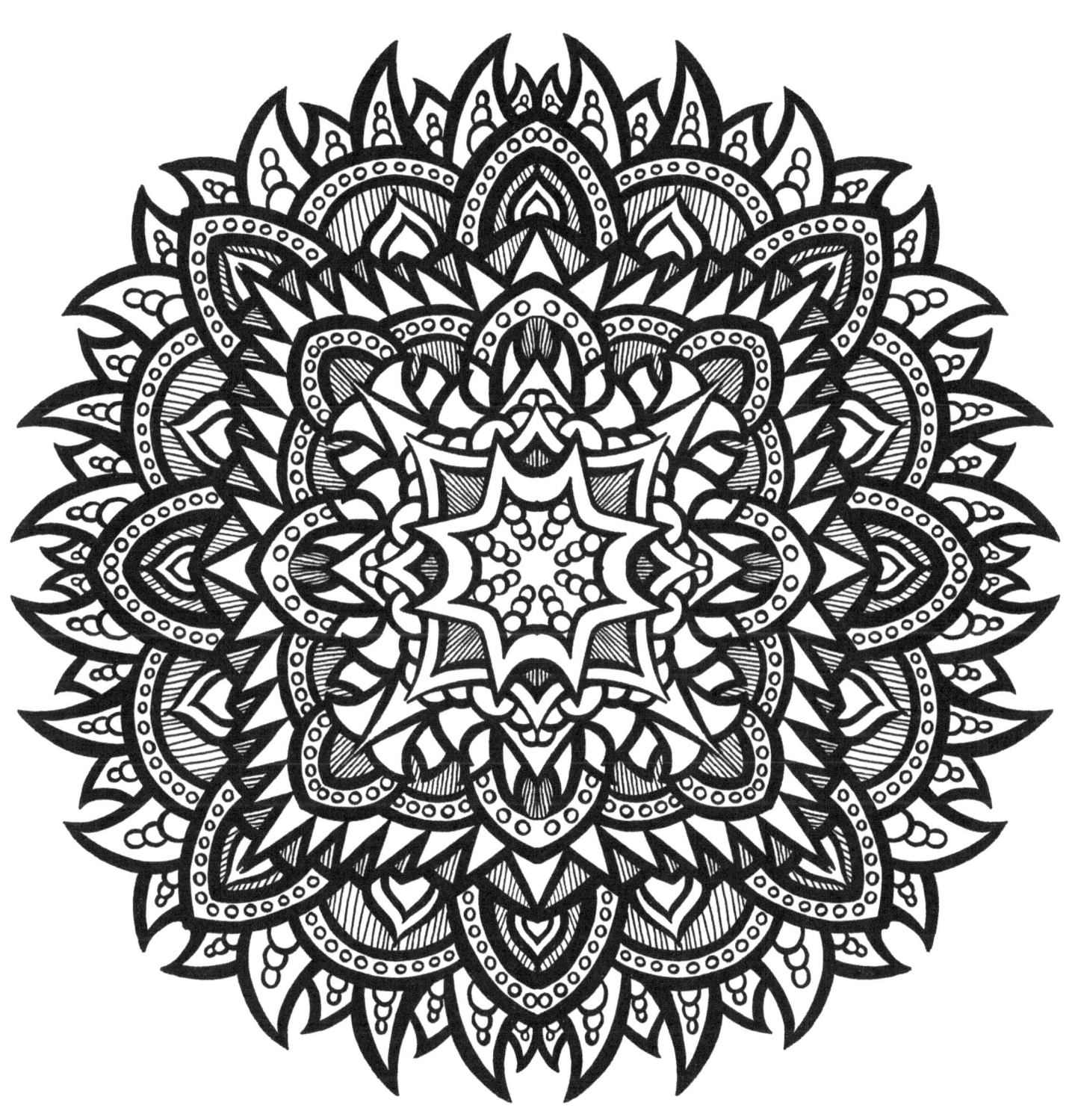

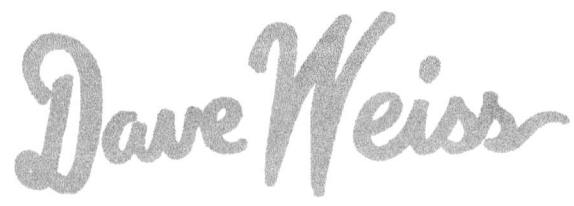

Kaleidoscopics Book 1
"Dangerous Beauty"

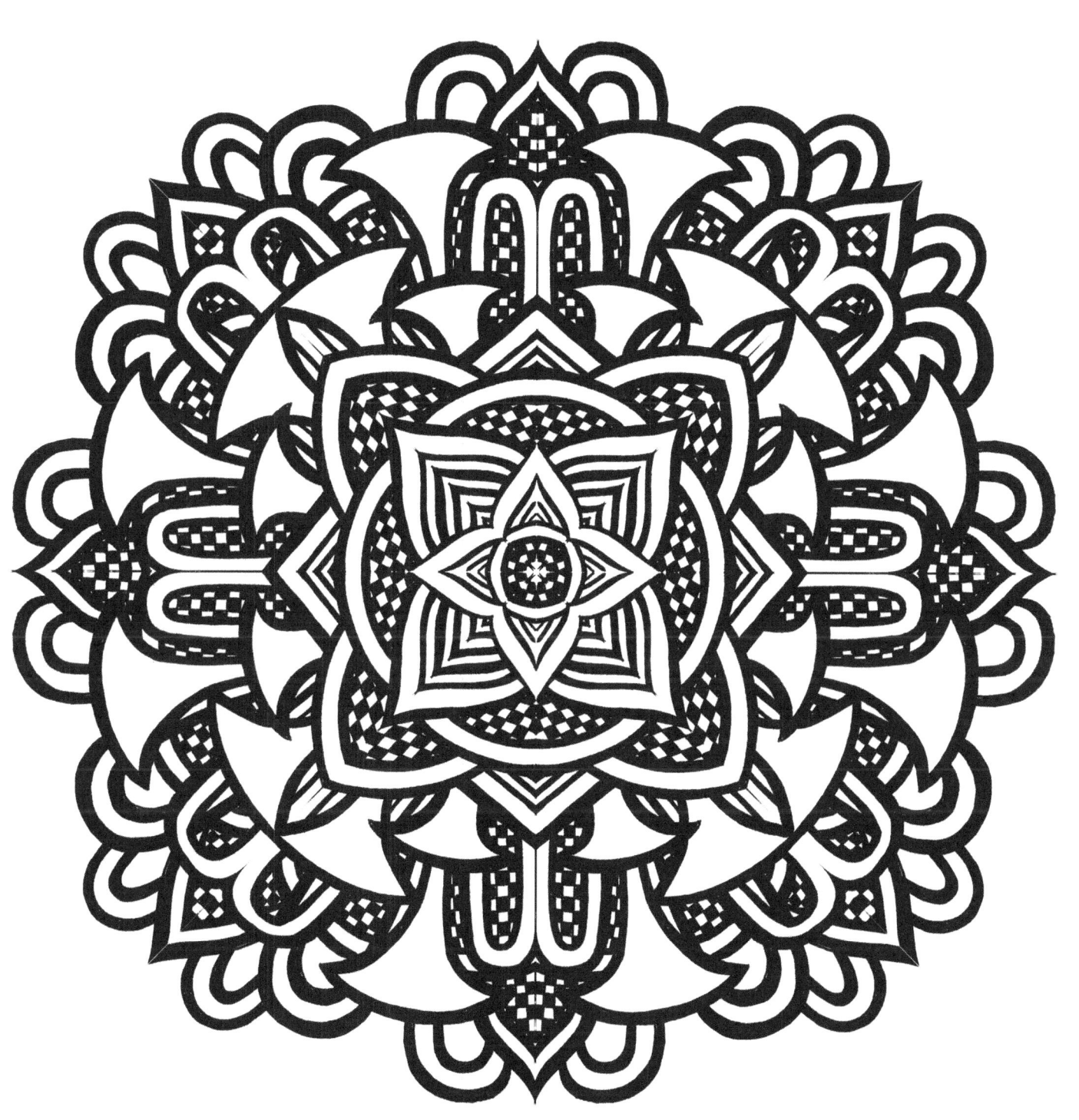

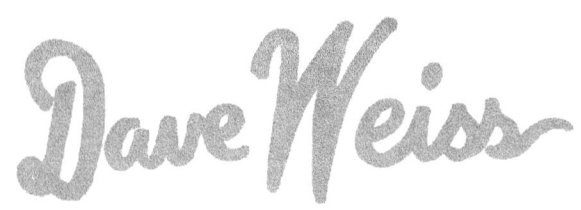

Kaleidoscopics Book 1
"24 Trombones"

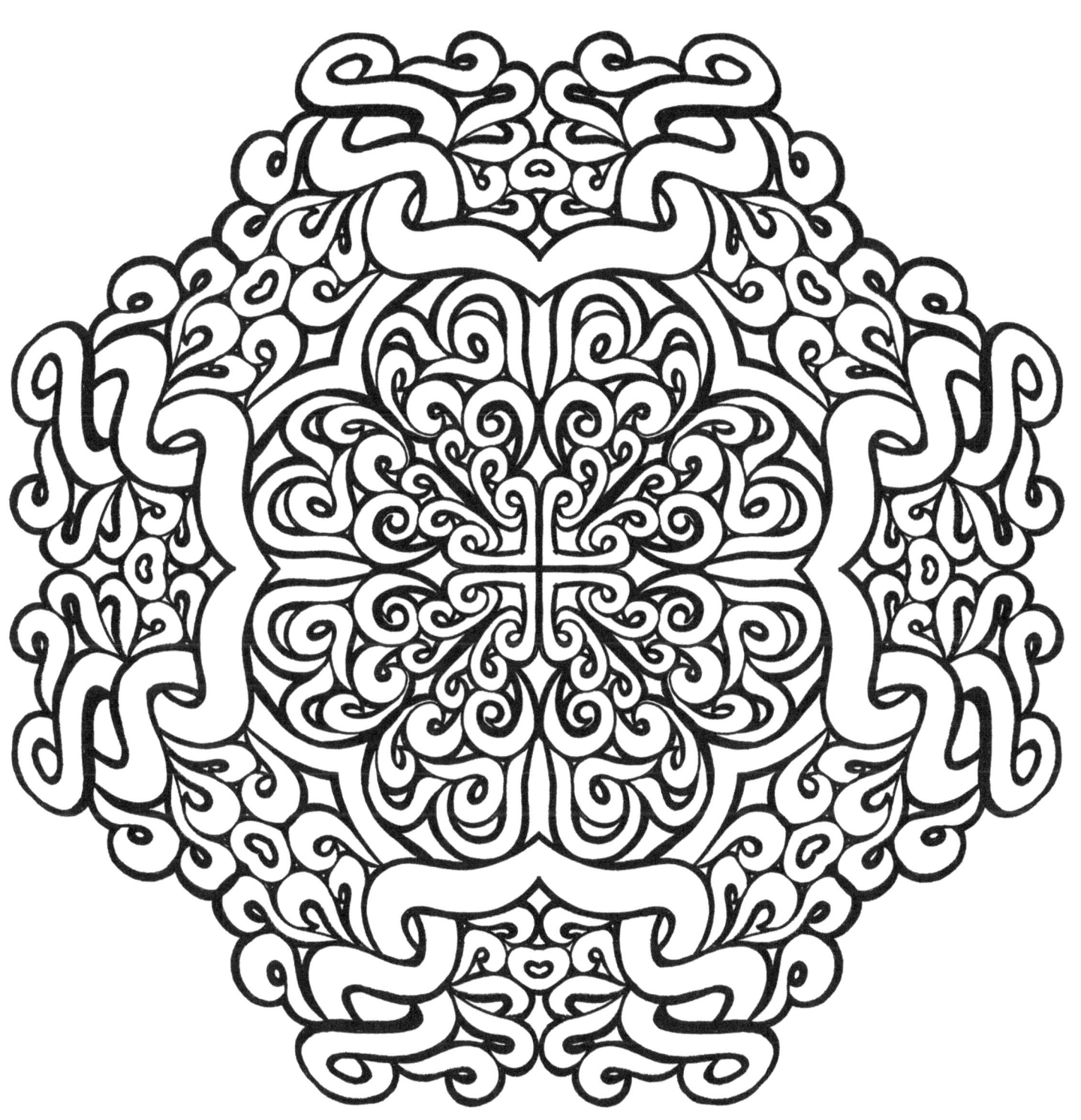

Dave Weiss

Kaleidoscopics Book 1
"Psychodelic Pathway"

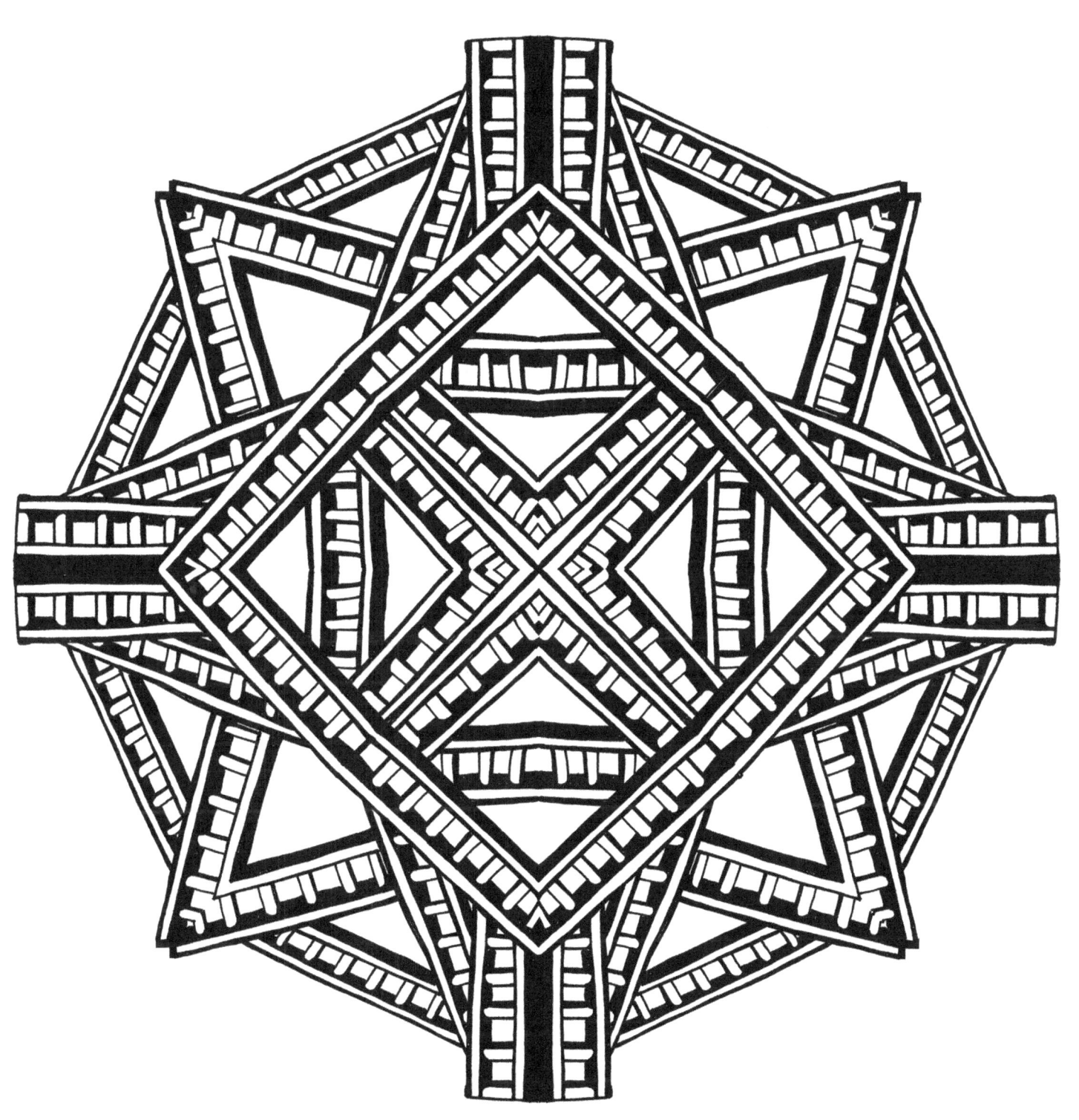

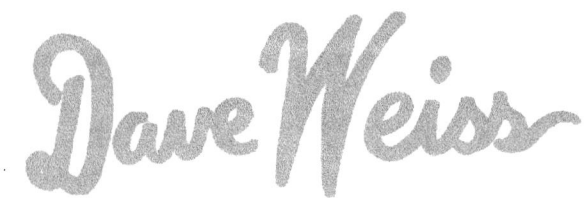

Kaleidoscopics Book 1
"Going Up"